Cambridge Elements

Elements in Crime Narratives
edited by
Margot Douaihy
Emerson College
Catherine Nickerson
Emory College of Arts and Sciences
Henry Sutton
University of East Anglia

INTERACTIVITY AND META-ENGAGEMENT IN DIGITAL MYSTERY NARRATIVES

Julialicia Case
University of Wisconsin, Green Bay

CAMBRIDGE
UNIVERSITY PRESS

Shaftesbury Road, Cambridge CB2 8EA, United Kingdom

One Liberty Plaza, 20th Floor, New York, NY 10006, USA

477 Williamstown Road, Port Melbourne, VIC 3207, Australia

314–321, 3rd Floor, Plot 3, Splendor Forum, Jasola District Centre, New Delhi – 110025, India

103 Penang Road, #05–06/07, Visioncrest Commercial, Singapore 238467

Cambridge University Press is part of Cambridge University Press & Assessment, a department of the University of Cambridge.

We share the University's mission to contribute to society through the pursuit of education, learning and research at the highest international levels of excellence.

www.cambridge.org
Information on this title: www.cambridge.org/9781009565288

DOI: 10.1017/9781009365895

© Julialicia Case 2026

This publication is in copyright. Subject to statutory exception and to the provisions of relevant collective licensing agreements, no reproduction of any part may take place without the written permission of Cambridge University Press & Assessment.

When citing this work, please include a reference to the DOI 10.1017/9781009365895

First published 2026

A catalogue record for this publication is available from the British Library

ISBN 978-1-009-56528-8 Hardback
ISBN 978-1-009-36587-1 Paperback
ISSN 2755-1873 (online)
ISSN 2755-1865 (print)

Cambridge University Press & Assessment has no responsibility for the persistence or accuracy of URLs for external or third-party internet websites referred to in this publication and does not guarantee that any content on such websites is, or will remain, accurate or appropriate.

For EU product safety concerns, contact us at Calle de José Abascal, 56, 1°, 28003 Madrid, Spain, or email eugpsr@cambridge.org

Interactivity and Meta-Engagement in Digital Mystery Narratives

Elements in Crime Narratives

DOI: 10.1017/9781009365895
First published online: January 2026

Julialicia Case
University of Wisconsin, Green Bay
Author for correspondence: Julialicia Case, casej@uwgb.edu

Abstract: This Element provides an in-depth analysis of digital mystery game narratives through the lens of game studies approaches, game design principles, and literary theory. Beginning with an overview of important game studies concepts, the Element argues that the narrative effects of video games cannot be fully understood without an understanding of these principles. Next, the Element incorporates these ideas into a detailed analysis of digital mystery stories, illustrating how game design elements augment and enhance narrative impact. Finally, the Element applies these principles to several print texts, illustrating how game studies principles help to articulate interactive strategies. Ultimately, this Element argues that incorporating digital mystery narratives into the field of crime studies goes beyond simply broadening the canon, but rather that an understanding of game studies principles has the potential to augment discussions of interactivity and reader participation in all crime narratives, regardless of media form.

Keywords: mystery narratives, video games, digital storytelling, game studies, empathy

© Julialicia Case 2026

ISBNs: 9781009565288 (HB), 9781009365871 (PB), 9781009365895 (OC)
ISSNs: 2755-1873 (online), 2755-1865 (print)

Contents

Introduction	1
Game Design Concepts and Crime Narratives	8
Environmental Storytelling and Empathy in *Gone Home* and *Firewatch*	26
Meaningful Choice, Implication, and Culpability in *Pentiment* and *Disco Elysium*	36
Blurred Boundaries, Cross-Cultural Connections, and Real-World Reflections in *Never Alone*, *Immortality*, and Transmedia Mysteries	46
Conclusions and Implications: What the Narrative Strategies of Digital Crime Narratives Mean for Storytelling	55
Works Cited	65

Introduction

Disco Elysium, ZA/UM's 2019 role-playing game, opens with a black screen, a strange voice, and a series of choices. Do you want to continue existing in darkness? Do you want to know more about the mysterious details of the world, such as your ex-wife? Which archetype would you prefer – Thinker, Sensitive, Physical, or something of your own creation? Eventually, you wake and find yourself to be a hungover, middle-aged white man, almost-naked, in a trashed hotel room. You learn that you are a police officer, who has been called to investigate a murder. You have a partner, Kim Kitsuragi, who is efficient, smart, and tolerant of your shortcomings. A body has been strung up in a tree outside, and you have important interviews to conduct and clues to examine. Unfortunately, you also have no memory of who you are or what has happened to bring you to this point in your life.

Disco Elysium – a game firmly ensconced in the noir detective tradition – was released to widespread acclaim, including four awards from the 2019 Game Awards, and a mention in *Time* magazine's top ten games of the decade. In Jordan Minor's 2021 review of the "Final Cut" edition, *PC Magazine* calls it "first and foremost an adult story," with "heady, literary density," claiming, "*Disco Elysium's* beating, thematic heart makes it the best PC game you can play at this moment in history" (Minor). Minor notes its roots in police procedurals, comparing it to contemporary television series such as *Bordertown* and *The Killing*, calling it "a solid murder mystery, full of clever twists and reversals [that is also] a pretense for the deeper investigation of the world itself and the sinister, yet familiar, social forces that shape it." On the game's official website, the developers cite inspirations such as *The Wire*, *True Detective*, and the fiction of Dashiell Hammett, marketing the game as "a detective RPG," with advertisements asking players, "What kind of cop are you" (*Disco Elysium*)?

Despite the success of the digital game, and widespread praise for its use of the crime story format, less well-known is the fact that *Disco Elysium* first began as a novel called *Sacred and Terrible Air*, which was published in Estonia by the game's creator, Robert Kurvitz in 2013. In an interview with Alex Wiltshire for *GamesRadar*, Kurvitz admits that the novel, which took him five years to write, was largely a failure, saying, "It sold 1,000 copies [and] after that I succumbed to deep alcoholism" (Wiltshire). In the wake of the failed novel project, novelist Kaur Kender approached Kurvitz with the idea of turning the story into a game. After considering the possibility, Kurvitz eventually reached out to the game's art director, Aleksander Rostov, saying purportedly, "My friend, we failed at so many things. Let us also fail at making a video game" (Wiltshire).

There are obviously many social and cultural forces at work in this example, including commercial, global, and industry influences that extend far beyond discussions of media. For the purposes of this Element, however, it is useful to begin with some questions about narrative form. In Wiltshire's interview, Kender explains his reasoning for making *Disco Elysium* as a video game, saying "My kids were telling me, 'Stop writing books! No one reads books! You should get into video games." In 2023 article for the *New York Times*, German Lopez notes, "about two-thirds of Americans, most of them adults, play video games. The video game industry was worth nearly $200 billion in 2021 – more than music, U.S. book publishing, and North American sports combined" (Lopez). As entertainment, video games are an evident cultural force, and the stories told through games are well known and beloved by audiences around the world. Despite this popularity, however, games still occupy a somewhat peripheral role in the realm of literary studies, often marked with concerns that games are somehow at odds with print literature, are harmful or escapist pastimes, or that the time players dedicate to digital games would be better spent engaging with more traditional literature. Games may be regarded as a danger to reading, a threat to academic programs centered on print-based narratives, or an administrative strategy to draw student interest, despite the clear evidence that game-based storytelling is evocative, memorable, and a widespread cultural force shaping discussions about storytelling and narrative on a massive, global scale.

In the fields of game studies and digital literary studies, discussions of narrative in video games have a long and developed tradition. Hartmut Koenitz's "What Game Narrative Are We Talking About? An Ontological Mapping of the Foundational Canon of Interactive Narrative Forms," offers a succinct overview of the history of narrative scholarship in video games, citing foundational scholars such as Espen Aarseth, Janet Murray, Jesper Juul, Gordon Calleja, Astrid Ensslin, Nick Montfort, Marie-Laure Ryan, and others. In the introduction to *Reading Digital Fiction: Narrative, Cognition, Mediality*, Alice Bell and Astrid Ensslin provide a concise overview of the strengths and limitations of three waves of theoretical scholarship focused on digital fiction, the first using poststructuralist models to examine hypertext fictions, the second focused on "the linguistic, narratological, multimodal, and/or interactive devices at work in a range of digital fictions" (6), and the third focused on data-driven reader response approaches, which Bell and Ensslin employ in their empirical examinations of five different generations of digital fiction in the rest of volume.

Although game studies scholars have long drawn from literary theoretical approaches and scholarship when examining and discussing digital narratives, these methodologies are often only part of a wider approach which also includes theoretical approaches from game design, media and film studies, and other areas, with the consensus being that the narrative effects of games cannot fully be understood through literary approaches alone. Even so, some game studies scholars argue that focusing on narrative in video games obscures and avoids crucial elements that are unique and central to games, as Ian Bogost argued famously in his 2017 *Atlantic* article, "Video Games Are Better Without Stories." In a critique of the *Last of Us* television remake, released in early 2023, Bogost writes, "I've long reasoned that no serious storyteller would select video games as their medium of choice, given how much better literature, cinema, and television are at narrative expression." Regardless of whether digital games can tell stories, or should tell stories, or do tell stories, the fact remains that games provide significant, memorable storytelling experiences for many people. And, in the case of *Disco Elysium*, the creators' choice to approach the story through a video game effectively transformed Harry Du Bois' explorations in Revachol from a story enjoyed by a handful of readers into an award-winning digital mystery narrative widely celebrated as one of the best of its time.

It is common and understandable for literary academic studies to approach video games through the lenses of literary critical theory, or through theoretical approaches rooted in media or game studies traditions. Despite the cultural force of video game storytelling and its widespread popularity and impact on audiences, however, the reverse approach is much less typical. If audiences are increasingly experiencing stories through video games – digital experiences with the capacity for narrative approaches that are more difficult to replicate in print text – how are digital game narratives shaping the broader expectations that audiences have for storytelling? What might the field of game studies have to offer literature? Could an understanding of game design techniques and game studies taxonomies, ontologies, and critical approaches assist literary scholars in more precisely identifying and articulating the interactive strategies at work in contemporary narratives? And how might those methods illuminate the stylistic approaches of contemporary print texts, which may be working to replicate or approximate the storytelling mechanisms and strategies easily afforded by digital media? These questions are the focus of this Element.

In no genre are these investigations more relevant than in the context of crime narratives. In *A Muse & A Maze: Writing as Puzzle, Mystery, and Magic*, Peter Turchi argues that writers of detective stories often take on the role of puzzle creators. From Turchi's perspective, "the classic detective story offers a world of answers and logic, a world in which problems can be not avoided, but solved" (52). Turchi differentiates the terms "puzzle" and "mystery," explaining that "most of the narratives commonly called 'mysteries' are, in fact, puzzles –

which is to say that everything we need to know can be known, and by the end of the story or novel is known. True mysteries are questions we are compelled to contemplate but cannot expect to answer with certainty" (52). In Turchi's view, all works of fiction have the capacity to work as puzzles, as authors lead readers along careful trails of discoveries and solutions. This perspective aligns with Tzvetan Todorov's classic definition of a whodunit as a novel containing "not one but two stories: the story of the crime and the story of the investigation" (139). From Turchi's perspective, the second story in a mystery narrative, the story of the detective solving the crime, is one of reader participation as readers work to interpret the clues and solve the case along with the detective.

In the 2011 article "The Appeal of the Mystery," philosopher Alan H. Goldman presents a developed argument for why the crime novel has long been one of the most popular genres of fiction among readers. Goldman considers different traditions in American and British mystery narratives and cites a variety of factors including morality, voyeurism, social criticism, and others. Most important, though, are Goldman's descriptions of narrative engagement. Like Turchi, Goldman notes the appeal of the puzzle, as readers attempt to piece together the clues alongside the detective. Goldman emphasizes the importance of cognitive engagement and empathetic connection to the detective character, but further emphasizes the similarities between games and the experience of mystery narratives, arguing,

> The detective's final narrative is not simply the solution to a complex puzzle, but an explanation of how it was solved, and the reader wins the competition with the author (or detective) to the extent that she anticipates that explanation in her ongoing interpretations ... This cognitive process requires attention to detail, inferential ability, memory, and imagination ... Only in the mystery novel is this interpretive process a competitive game. It comes to a head when the detective announces that he knows the answer to the crime puzzle but delays revealing it, challenging the reader to complete the interpretive process. (266)

Goldman argues that "the reader is cognitively engaged on every page, seeking ordered narrative patterns in textual data" (266). In this way, mystery narratives are appealing not only because of the puzzle elements, but also because readers are tasked with interpreting details alongside the detective – indeed, going further to slip into the persona of the detective, to adopt their worldview, knowledge and perspectives – and creating and revising their own stories about what might have happened.

Goldman begins his article by acknowledging the ways that mystery narratives are often dismissed as "merely part of popular culture, not true literary works of art" (261) and "'escapist' literature ... worth no more aesthetically than mindless television fare" (261), critiques which have been, at times, applied to contemporary video games. Though Goldman does not discuss game design or video games specifically in his article, his description of the appeal of mystery narratives touches on many components that could equally be applied to discussions of video game storytelling, namely that readers/players slip into the skin of a detective character, viewing the world through their eyes, and actively creating and revising a narrative as they attempt to craft the actual story of the crime before the detective does. Goldman's assertion that game elements are a key reason why audiences read crime fiction not only emphasizes the importance that critical analysis of digital mystery games holds for scholarship of crime narratives as a whole, but further suggests that an understanding of game design, specifically the ways that storytelling happens within digital games, will illuminate discussions of the ways that mystery narratives work, regardless of media form.

In the article "Designing the Mystery: Elision and Exegesis in Games," Clara Fernández-Vara, a game studies theorist and game designer, discusses narrative game design in video game mysteries. She notes that for game designers the process of "leaving gaps invites the reader of the mystery, as well as the game player, to think of ways to fill them, thus activating the participatory qualities of the digital medium including videogames" (51). Fernández-Vara highlights the concepts of elision and exegesis in digital mysteries, noting that:

> *Elision* can ... be a powerful tool in narrative game design by omitting information so that the player can find it or infer it. By extension, *exegesis* (i.e. interpretation of a text) can be another key game design tool by requiring players to interpret and explain a story that is presented in fragments, ambiguously, or from diverging points of view. (52)

Fernández-Vara notes that this participatory process is true for a variety of media, including print mysteries narratives. She explains that "one of the issues in discussing stories in games is that they are referred to in terms of telling, as if the process of storytelling was univocal and where the content is communicated one-way" (56). Instead Fernández-Vara emphasizes the role that players and readers contribute to creating a story, saying, "I prefer to invoke the term *storybuilding* in the context of games because it refers to both the craft of creating the pieces of the story on the part of the creator and the process of reconstruction that players have to carry out" (56). Fernández-Vara's article illustrates that while this process is common in digital game narratives, it is also a key factor in print mysteries, highlighting the capacity for game design techniques to illuminate narrative strategies beyond digital media.

While it might be tempting to limit the application of game design concepts to mystery narratives, or other stories with overt puzzle elements, Turchi explains the importance of understanding mystery narrative strategies more broadly, outside the specific limits of the genre. He contrasts the specific narrative puzzles of crime narratives with the larger mysteries of existence. These mysteries are ultimately unsolvable, but the promise of discovering insight into humanity is what draws many readers to fiction. Turchi argues that:

> Every well-constructed piece of fiction has elements of a puzzle, and every piece of fiction that means to provoke readers to a state of wonder or contemplation has at least some element of mystery. The meeting of art and actuality, or artifice and reality, can be seen as the combination of the strategic arrangement of information and the acknowledgment of true, unsolvable mysteries. (57)

While, many readers of whodunit crime narratives may come to a work with anticipations about the form and its conventions, so that "a narrative built on the basic framework of a detective story ... is in conversation with the reader's expectations" (Turchi 71), and while Todorov argues that successful detective fiction "is not the one that transgresses the rules of the genre, but the one which conforms to them" (138), mystery narratives are not the only forms with such expectations. In Turchi's view, most works of fiction – and crime narratives, in particular – are similar to games in the ways that authors must develop a careful puzzle, one that is satisfying, surprising, and often in-keeping with the larger conventions of a genre or form.

The mystery narrative genre is diverse and varied, meaning that discussions of puzzles and solutions may not always be relevant to narrative experience, as in the case of noir detective fiction, with its traditional emphasis on institutional corruption, nihilism, and psychological instability, where complexities of morality and victimhood often make the task of assigning blame difficult or impossible. In the chapter "Playing with Negativity: *Max Payne*, Neoliberal Collapse, and the Noir Video Game," from the 2020 anthology *Noir Affect*, Brian Rejack explores the experience of affect in the *Max Payne* noir video game series, describing the ways in which the game experiences push players to engage with the noir perspective, either by participating with the internal systems of the game, or by resisting them through the use of game modifications or other tools. Rejack notes that "If you're skilled enough at the game, then you get the happy ending. Playing the game well is at odds with the production of noir affect in the player" (186). In other words, regardless of the narrative events of the story, players can influence the emotional experience of the world based on how they engage with the game.

Rejack particularly highlights the ways that employing the use of game modifications – downloadable content produced by independent programmers – can allow players to push back against a game's emotional experience or content, with the potential of encouraging players to resist or adapt the affect of a game experience. Rejack argues that with modifications,

> the game is not *played*, so much as *played with*. It becomes a software playground in which one can jump meaninglessly and create sonic atmospheres for the sheer aesthetic pleasure of so doing ... It represents a playing with the material that makes up noir affect. The affect can still be experienced, but in this altered form of play, it disrupts the cultural logics that would enable a specific circumscribed form of response to it. (192)

Rejack's argument highlights the importance of considering player behavior and media theory in addition to game design and game studies principles when analyzing digital mystery narratives. In Mia Consalvo's foundational book, *Cheating: Gaining Advantage in Videogames*, she uses Gérard Genette's concept of paratext to describe the impact that external elements such as "gaming magazines, strategy guides, mod chip makers, ... other companies, and industry segments work to shape the game play experience in particular ways" (9). Both Rejack and Consalvo illustrate how paratextual elements can contribute significantly to a game's experience in ways that may not be immediately apparent in an inherent analysis of the game. Video game crime stories often encourage players to experience and participate in a narrative, but they also afford players the opportunity to join in a digital world, engaging with (or resisting) its affective experience, simply existing within the larger world of a mystery, much in the way that noir novels do, and providing the opportunity for a variety of experiences and goals.

In this way, an examination of digital mystery narratives relies on a detailed consideration of the elements of game design and game studies concepts relevant to a given game. Further, the similarities that scholars such as Turchi, Fernández-Vara, and Goldman have noted between mystery narratives and game experiences suggest that an understanding of game design principles has direct relevance to a more thorough understanding of mystery narrative experience even in more traditional print forms. In this Element, I will first introduce common game design principles useful for understanding how games work and how they are constructed. In the subsequent sections, I will explore the ways that game design principles operate in tandem with traditional crime narrative elements in digital games by examining the narrative strategies in the digital games, *Disco Elysium*, *Gone Home*, *Firewatch*, and *Pentiment*. From there, I will move to larger discussions of the ways that these strategies have the potential to foster cross-cultural connection and encourage players to empathize with experiences and characters that may differ from their own. I will end the media analysis portion by discussing some examples of transmedia mystery narratives, where game design strategies rely on collective intelligence, encouraging players to interact with one another and contribute to the story, effectively blurring the boundaries between the game world and the physical one.

Because digital games amplify the sense of reader participation and engagement that is often present in many crime narratives in the ways that Goldman and Fernández-Vara describe, an understanding of game design principles is useful for articulating the narrative strategies of the genre regardless of form. Critical analysis of video games is crucial given the widespread popularity of digital games and the increasing tendency for audiences to turn to games for narrative experiences. It is tempting to view the literary study of video games as a simple broadening of the canon, allowing digital stories into the fold by approaching them through the traditional lenses of literary criticism. An analysis of video game narratives is incomplete without game design principles and game studies approaches, which are vital to fully understanding these narrative experiences. More importantly, in the case of crime narratives, which, as I have explained, share much in common with games, games studies principles can help to articulate key features of narrative experience, even in traditional print narratives, as I will demonstrate in the last section of this Element. As audiences become increasingly accustomed to the narrative experiences that digital games make possible, it is likely that this will fundamentally alter our expectations for how stories work and what they can do, meaning that a firm understanding of game studies is not merely useful for the analysis of digital games, but also increasingly essential to an understanding of narrative in all media forms, particularly in the study of mystery and crime narratives.

Game Design Concepts and Crime Narratives

An understanding of the structural and critical frameworks that are unique to game design and game studies is crucial to the analysis of digital games. Thus, this Element will begin with a brief overview of important game studies concepts and the unique experiences that they impart to narrative. Koenitz gives a concise account of the major theorists and critical approaches that characterized the beginning of video game analysis, noting with particular surprise that discussions about the definition of what a narrative is and what comprises it were largely absent from early theoretical dialogues, despite the interdisciplinary origins of the field. Koenitz explains:

> When scholars originate in different traditions, there is a danger of misunderstanding, as the respective terms and underlying categorical concepts are not

automatically understood. This is especially problematic when, at first glance, the vocabulary appears to be identical, yet no attempt was made to establish a shared understanding of the word field around narrative. (2)

In the context of this Element, it is worth acknowledging the challenges of cross-disciplinary discussions, particularly those with a shared vocabulary, and recognizing that the expectations and assumptions about what a narrative is and how it operates can vary widely across academic disciplines and genres. A complete summary of games studies concepts and approaches is far beyond the scope of this project, but I hope in this section to provide a comprehensive overview of several foundational concepts, and to illustrate how an understanding of how narrative operates in digital mystery games can broaden the ways in which narrative is defined and examined within literary studies, illuminating the field in important ways.

Early game studies discourse tended to focus on debates about how best to engage critically with video games, discussions which still characterize the field, to some extent, even now. Bell and Ensslin's 2024 book, *Reading Digital Fiction: Narrative, Cognition, Mediality*, begins with an overview of what the authors define as six generations of digital fiction and three waves of scholarship, noting that in "the first wave of scholarship, readers were ... often situated in a binary relationship with their print counterparts ... with digital writing conceptualized as something that would liberate the reader" (5). Often referred to as the ludology-narratology debate, early discussions about digital games in the realm of literary studies often came from narratologists, such as Janet Murray who argued in *Hamlet on the Holodek* in 1997 that digital, fully immersive storytelling experiences were "the most powerful sensory illusion imaginable" (26). At the same time, ludologists such as Espen Aarseth argued that an understanding of the narrative experiences afforded by digital games was incomplete without a discussion of the unique elements only possible in games. In Aarseth's seminal work, *Cybertexts: Perspectives on Ergodic Literature*, also published in 1997, he claims that:

> A search for traditional literary values in texts that are neither intended nor structured as literature will only obscure the unique aspects of these texts ... If these texts redefine literature by expanding our notion of it ... then they must also redefine what is literary, and therefore they cannot be measured by an old, unmodified aesthetics. (22)

From the perspective of ludologists, literary studies, though relevant to examinations of digital narrative, is insufficient for examining and discussing the unique narrative effects of this kind of storytelling.

Though less central to contemporary game studies scholarship, the context of the ludology-narratology debate is still important for understanding how debates focused on ontology, approach, perspective, and lexicon still characterize the field today. Bell and Ensslin categorize the second wave of digital fiction research as one focused on "applying replicable analytical tools and frameworks to individual digital fiction works" (6), by examining elements such as interactivity, voice, immersion, and perspective. Like Aarseth and Koenitz, Bell and Ensslin note the presence of implicit bias and limited perspective in these examinations, which, "inevitably present a necessarily limited point of view, driven by the analyst's individual biases and theoretical lenses" (6). Ultimately Bell and Ensslin underscore the importance of the third wave of digital fiction scholarship, where "scholars seek to empirically investigate digital fiction reading by collecting and analyzing reader responses to individual texts using both qualitative and quantitative data collection methods" (6). Their book's introduction highlights the ways that studies of digital narrative and the critical approaches to it are in flux and constantly evolving. In the introduction to Aubrey Anable's 2018 book, *Playing With Feelings: Video Games and Affect*, for instance, she laments the binary divisions she sees in critical approaches to video games, expressing the hope that applying affect theory to video games will allow her to "read across code, images, and bodies without reducing video games to either their representational qualities or their digital and mechanical properties" (xvi). Anable's concern that critical game studies may limit the capacity for scholars to talk about subjects such as emotion, representation, and physicality helps to illustrate how much of the field is still unexplored and changing, and how, despite the efforts of Koenitz and others to classify ontologies, lexicons, and theoretical approaches, scholars are still in the process of interrogating and refining interdisciplinary critical approaches while also navigating a rapidly evolving industry.

In the remainder of this section, I give an overview of several important game design concepts and game studies critical approaches. Brevity requires that this is neither an exhaustive list, nor one that engages fully with the substantial debates and discussions centering these concepts. I have done my best to acknowledge complexities and counter-perspectives when possible, but my hope is that this discussion will provide a comprehensive overview accessible to literary scholars who may not be familiar with these concepts and will act as a portal for further exploration.

One of the earliest debates central to the field of game studies is the question, "What is a game?" and the concept of the magic circle is one of the most interesting examples of the ways that games can lead to compelling narrative experiences that might be challenging to replicate in other media forms. First introduced by Johan Huizinga, a Dutch historian, in his classic text *Homo Ludens: A Study of the Play-Element in Culture*, the term magic circle refers to the ways in which game spaces are unique in that they allow shared cultural experiences, with rules and goals that exist outside of the everyday workings of society. Games and play operate by social contract, where players abide by rules specifically for the purpose of enjoying the pleasure of a game, an experience which often has no larger consequences to the world outside of it. Huizinga argues that playing a game is a "free activity standing quite consciously outside 'ordinary' life as being 'not serious,' but at the same time absorbing the players intensely and utterly ... It proceeds within its own proper boundaries of time and space according to fixed rules and in an orderly manner. It promotes the formation of social groupings, which tend to ... stress their difference from the common world" (32). In a game of soccer, for instance, players are aware that play must take place within the confines of a designated field, that they must abide by rules such as avoiding touching the ball with their hands, and that "success" within the world of the game means maneuvering the ball into a net more times than their opponent. While professional games of soccer can certainly result in monetary and celebrity gain, the result of most casual games of soccer have little impact on the outside world.

In the book *Rules of Play: Game Design Fundamentals*, Katie Salen Tekinbas and Eric Zimmerman discuss the ways in which the magic circle has the potential to transform the everyday world in powerful ways. They note, "within the magic circle, special meanings accrue and cluster around objects and behaviors. In effect, a new reality is created, defined by the rules of the game and inhabited by its players" (107). Indeed, one of the most interesting elements of the concept of the magic circle is its porousness and the capacity for the game world to shape the real one. Beat Suter notes that "when we speak of the framing dimension of the game, we point to the ... delimitation to the real world. Where does the game world stop and where does reality begin? Or where does reality cease, and where does the virtuality of the game begin" (21). Miguel Sicart writes that contemporary technology shapes users' experiences of the world, regardless of games or storytelling, arguing that "we don't need games to create a world. Computers create worlds in which our experience and subjectivity is affected by their mediation and agency" (55). Regardless of how one defines the magic circle, or characterizes its impact, from a narrative perspective, storytelling experiences in games are unique in that they may encourage players to act in ways they might not normally, and to challenge rules and conventions in the everyday world. In the social deduction game, *Werewolves*, for instance, players might accuse one another of lying, comment overtly on body posture or speech patterns, or subvert social hierarchies by voting out players who occupy positions of authority outside the game. These experiences may occasionally lead to hurt feelings in the moment, particularly if players feel frustrated or if debates become heated, but generally these disagreements have little lasting consequence outside of the game. Further, the magic circle can provide a space apart, where players are more willing to sit with concepts that might make them uncomfortable otherwise, or to engage with those ideas in new ways.

In Tracy Fullerton's *Game Design Workshop: A Playcentric Approach to Creating Innovative Games,* game designer Brenda Romero tells a story about designing a game with her seven-year-old daughter to help her understand the emotional complexities of the Middle Passage, an event crucial to her child's heritage. Romero's daughter comes home from school, explaining "the Middle Passage with a memory that would have made any parent or teacher proud, naming names and citing key moments in abolition. What was missing however, was any sense of emotion or connection" (89). Together, the two design an impromptu game based on the Middle Passage, using an index card and painted tokens. It is only then, as they are playing the game and making choices about food and boat capacity, that Romero's daughter "stared at the boat for a bit, the opposing shores on the opposite side of the table and finally asked, 'Did this really happen, Mommy?'" (89). Romero credits her daughter's emotional connection to the Middle Passage to the concept of the magic circle, arguing that "after Black History Month at school, after movies, after books, after posters, after lectures, it was finally the mechanics of a simple and spontaneous game and the time she took to experience it (the time in the 'magic circle') that brought the connection home. They day ended with our family discussing the Middle Passage at length and on a very personal level" (89).

Romero's anecdote emphasizes the potential that the magic circle offers to encourage players to engage deeply with the content of a game narrative. When players participate in a game, they willingly adopt its rules, restrictions, and boundaries, and they are often asked to take on a role or a viewpoint that is different from the one they inhabit in day-to-day life. Within a game experience, typical social codes may be upended, or hierarchies subverted; players may be asked to take on roles that are unfamiliar to them or even at odds with their preferred perspectives. Because a game space is seen as playful, fun, and temporary, with little lasting impact on the outside world, players willingly participate in this "altered" world, and as a result, they can be more open to engaging with and adopting unfamiliar or uncomfortable standpoints. As a mechanism for communication, the magic circle offers the opportunity for game storytelling experiences to be profound and meaningful, pushing participants to engage deeply with emotional perspectives which might otherwise be unfamiliar, difficult, or uncomfortable.

One of the primary mechanisms that enable games to encourage players to connect with a narrative in significant ways and foster emotional connection is through the concept of meaningful choice. Sid Meier's oft-cited and foundational quote from *Game Architecture and Design* by Andrew Rollings and Dave Morris claims "a game is a series of interesting choices" (61). For many game design and game studies scholars, choice is crucial to game design, ensuring that each playthrough of any given game is unique and reliant on the actions and decisions of a specific set of players. In *Cybertext*, Aarseth differentiates the narrative experiences possible in ergodic literature from those of more traditional narratives, stating:

> A reader [of a traditional text], however strongly engaged in the unfolding of a narrative, is powerless ... like a passenger on a train, he can study and interpret the shifting landscape, he may rest his eyes wherever he pleases, even release the emergency brake and step off, but he is not free to move the tracks in a different direction. He cannot have the player's pleasure of influence. (4)

For Aarseth, choice and influence are a crucial difference between game experiences and those in more traditional print texts. Because players are often active participants in game narratives, permitted to shape and influence those stories, they feel a much deeper connection and sense of responsibility to and ownership of them. This close connection between player and narrative allows games to have a potent impact, one that is very different from stories told in more traditional forms. Definitions of what constitutes a meaningful choice and how to design one in a game are varied and beyond the scope of this Element, but for the purposes of illustrating how crime narrative games might effectively utilize this approach, we can define a meaningful choice as one where players are aware that their actions and decisions in a game influence the story. Further, the impact of a meaningful choice has lasting consequences on the narrative, resulting in a significant influence that persists throughout the story, and is permanent, with lasting consequences.

A strong example of the ways that meaningful choice might influence a crime narrative is Dontnod Entertainment's 2015 game, *Life Is Strange*. In this game, players take on the role of teenager Max Caulfield, a high school photography student who learns at the beginning of the game that she has the power to rewind time. In an early scene in the game, Max discovers her new ability when she saves her friend Chloe Price from being shot and killed by another student in the school bathroom. Max's abilities enable her to rewind and replay conversations, altering and adjusting her responses to incorporate new information or to inspire new responses. Her powers are limited temporally, however; although players can rewind and replay most conversations as many times as they like, once they have finished a particular conversation, they are unable to go back to it, and the story moves forward with the consequences of those choices. Though players have some influence on the storyline in the game, most meaningful choice elements in *Life Is Strange* are centered on the relationships the player constructs between Max and the other characters. Players have a great deal of influence for instance, on the romantic overtones of Max's friendship with Chloe, and the degree to which Max chooses to learn about the students, faculty, and members of her community. As a result, players often feel a sense of responsibility toward the other characters and a close connection to them. Lurking in the background of these relationships, however, is the deeper threat of Rachel Amber's mysterious disappearance. Players discover Rachel's body at the end of the game and learn she was a victim of a photography instructor who often drugged female students to take nonconsensual sexual photos of them. The underlying mystery of Rachel Amber heightens the stakes of Max's relationship building, as players hurry to protect and learn more about the others around them.

Early in the game, another student, Kate Marsh, reeling from bullying that has resulted from sexual photos that were released after her run-in with this photographer, attempts suicide. Players must attempt to talk her out of her choice, and their success in doing so is reliant on the degree to which they have supported Kate and learned about her character in the game thus far. It is possible to succeed or fail in rescuing Kate, and the narrative continues regardless, with Max either mourning her death or checking in during her recovery in the hospital. This choice is meaningful in that it has a drastic and immediate impact on the game's storyline, but even more, the player's ability to save Kate is closely linked to the degree in which Max has engaged with her, by building and nurturing the relationship. Regardless of how the encounter plays out, this narrative approach makes it likely that players will feel a close emotional connection to Kate, along with a lasting sense of responsibility, care, and connection. Further, from a mystery narrative perspective, it also asks players to engage directly with the central crime. Players are not distant observers, but instead active participants in a world where an ominous menace threatens their friendships, the connections they have worked hard to build. Although players are unaware of the link between Kate's suicide and Rachel's disappearance at the time of Kate's suicide attempt, asking players to learn about her experiences, and providing drastic consequences for not doing so pushes players to learn more about the mystery at the heart of the game, and to develop a deep, personal investment in solving it.

Beyond being a strong example of the ways that meaningful choice can push players to feel a sense of responsibility and investment in a story, Kate's suicide attempt is also an excellent example of the impact of failure and replay, another element of game design that is important to consider in understanding the ways that digital game experiences might augment and enhance existing interactive elements of mystery narratives. In the book *The Art of Failure: An Essay on the Pain of Playing Video Games*, Jesper Juul describes the "paradox of failure in games" (2), observing "that we generally try to avoid the unpleasant emotions that we get from hearing about a sad event or failing at a task. Yet we actively seek out these emotions in stories, art, and games" (4). For Juul, failing is integral to the enjoyment of games, as players are often frustrated if a game is too simple. Further, failure is often a more personal experience in games, with players tending to feel a great deal of responsibility for their inadequacies. Juul writes:

> When you fail in a game, it really means that *you* were in some way inadequate. Such a feeling of inadequacy is unpleasant for us, and it is odd that we choose to subject ourselves to it. However, while games uniquely induce such feelings of being inadequate, they also motivate us to play *more* in order to escape the same inadequacy, and the feeling of escaping failure (often by improving our skills) is central to the enjoyment of games. Games promise us a fair chance of redeeming ourselves. This distinguishes game failure from failure in our regular lives: (good) games are designed such that they give us a fair chance, whereas the regular world makes no such promises. (7)

In Juul's view, failure in games is crucial because it encourages players to replay an experience again and again with the promise that they might one day succeed, and this promise of success in the face of failure is something that draws players to games because it is an uncommon experience in the everyday world.

In the example of Kate Marsh's suicide attempt in *Life Is Strange*, failure makes it more likely that players will play the game repeatedly, engaging with the world again and again. If players fail at saving Kate, they may want to replay the game to see if they are able to succeed in a subsequent playthrough. Even if they succeed on the first attempt, players may be motivated to play the game again to see how failing alters the storyline. *Life Is Strange* is packed with meaningful choices, repeatedly asking players to make decisions without allowing them to predict how their selections may influence the story. In this way, the story is crafted from countless moments of potential failure, and with every choice, players feel even more responsible for the characters and the narrative events.

Do you try to improve Max's friendship with the local bully? Do you encourage her to develop romantic feelings for Chloe? How much is Max willing to sacrifice for the safety of her town? Further, the game also incorporates an achievement mechanic, where players are encouraged to explore the world by taking photographs to fill in the blanks in Max's journal. Missing a photograph is another potential failure that might push a player to replay the game in an effort to fully complete the journal. As Juul describes in *The Art of Failure*, failure in *Life Is Strange* can easily feel personal. If someone fails to save Kate, for instance, they may feel that they did not engage with her character sufficiently. Similarly, if a player misses a photograph, it is likely they will fault themselves for not exploring the world fully enough. The sense of personal investment and agency afforded by failure and replay help to create narrative experiences that ask players to take responsibility for a story and their own role in crafting it, an effect which helps to make stories in games and digital experience feel personal, meaningful, and memorable.

The concept of failure in *Life Is Strange* also illustrates a further element of digital games that can add a sense of influence and agency to a narrative experience. Beyond shaping the events of the story, meaningful choice in the game is important in that it enables to players to influence the central character, an experience which provides a much closer connection to character than might be possible in other media. Beyond affecting the events of the story, players are actively shaping Max's character, considering the values that are important to her while also evaluating their own. One of the most central narrative choices in *Life Is Strange* is the degree to which players will encourage Max to develop romantic feelings for Chloe or her friend Warren. Depending on the choices players make, Max has the option at various points in the story to kiss both characters. Although Chloe occupies a much more central role in the story than Warren, which makes it more likely that players will make choices that lead to romance between the two women, romantic and platonic relationships are possible with both characters within the narrative. The events of the story are similar regardless of how players choose to develop Max's character, but allowing players the opportunity to shape key elements of Max's personality, such as her romantic interests, makes it likely that players will feel a close connection to and investment in her character.

In *Rules of Play: Game Design Fundamentals*, Tekinbas and Zimmerman explain the difference between embedded and emergent narrative elements, definitions which are particularly important when considering player relationships to character development. According to Tekinbas and Zimmerman, "embedded narrative is pre-generated narrative content that exists prior to a player's interaction with the game … it is experienced through player interaction but exists formally apart from it" (7). Embedded narrative elements are components of a game experience which are the same regardless of player choice and approach. In *Life Is Strange*, for instance, all players will experience certain narrative moments regardless of the choices they make. In every playthrough of the game, Max discovers her ability to rewind time while witnessing Chloe being shot in the high school bathroom. Regardless of the choices players make about romantic involvement, Chloe and Max's friendship develops throughout the game. Max always learns that her newfound powers come with serious consequences, such as the storm that threatens Arcadia Bay at the end of the game. In contrast, Tekinbas and Zimmerman explain that:

> not all narrative in games takes the form of pre-generated, embedded content. Narrative can also be emergent, which means that it arises from the set of rules governing interaction with the game system. Unlike embedded narrative, emergent narrative elements arise during play from the complex system of the game, often in unexpected ways. Most moment-to-moment play in a game is emergent, as player choice leads to unpredictable narrative experiences. (7)

The concept of emergence is particularly important when considering character development. While the narrative events in *Life Is Strange* are similar regardless of playthrough, key components of Max's character often emerge through player choice and action, and because they are the compilation of the accretion of many small choices made throughout the game, it can be difficult for any two playthroughs of the game to unfold in exactly the same manner. In this way, meaningful choice and failure are closely linked to character development, as, often, player's agency in a game narrative is most evident in the ways that their choices and interactions have shaped and influenced the central character.

In *Craft in the Real World*, Matt Salesses discusses the ways that authorial choices about conflict and characterization contribute to broader cultural messages within a work, often reinforcing colonial perspectives, or other types of problematic systemic discrimination. Salesses argues that "the story arc is always read together with the character arc to create meaning . . . And the writer is better off if she is aware of the ways in which she participates in and creates meaning – so that she can mean things more consciously and conscientiously" (66–67). In the case of a game like *Life Is Strange*, although players have an impact on character development, and an effect on the narrative, these influences are limited in that players can only experience what has already been coded into the game. In other words, if players choose to develop Max's feelings for Chloe and deepen the romance between them, this is only because it is permitted (and encouraged) within the game to begin with. Digital games do allow players a great deal of agency, but these emergent elements are still generally constrained by the limits of the game, and though a variety of character and story arcs may be possible, they are still ultimately bounded by the visions of the creators.

The concept of embedded and emergent narrative elements is also important to the discussion of another component significant to fiction in digital games: environmental storytelling. As in traditional print narratives, stories in games take place in a specific setting, but unlike print narratives, players are often given a great deal of freedom in the ways that they engage with the world and the paths that they take within it. In the opening of *Life Is Strange*, for instance, after Max has discovered her newfound ability to rewind time, she expresses the desire to hurry back to the bathroom to see if she can stop Chloe's murder. Players can choose to rush back to the bathroom immediately, or they can take their time, engaging with the setting, exploring the classroom, examining the posters in the hallway, or speaking with characters nearby. The story continues in the same way regardless of how much time players spend exploring the world, with the only difference being that players who spend time exploring the setting learn more about the context for the story, an investment that often rewards them with satisfying narrative experiences. Players who explore Kate's room in detail, for instance, are more likely to be able to avert her suicide attempt, and players who spend time exploring the world are more likely to create connections with other characters and fill in all the photographs in Max's journal. Allowing players to interact with the environment and giving them substantial freedom in the ways in which they explore and examine the setting contributes a great to deal to the storytelling experience.

In *Rules of Play*, Tekinbas and Zimmerman note the

> interdependent relationship between the fictive world and story events. The events of the plot, the "game story," are made possible by the existence of a larger fictional world in which the story takes place. At the same time, the story events themselves help to flesh out and inform the fictive world ... Together these two elements of game narratives create an artificial context where game experience acquires narrative meaning. (26)

In this way, exploration of the world can be seen as a key component of the narrative experience of digital games, even in moments when that exploration does not seem to contribute to or inform the embedded elements of the plot. Even if a player chooses to ignore Chloe's predicament at the beginning of *Life Is Strange*, electing instead to examine the objects in the classroom and engage with the other students, for instance, those emergent experiences still contribute to the narrative in that they deepen the player's connection to the world, their understanding of its elements, and their sense of agency within it.

This is particularly true with games where components of the world reward exploration by offering narrative details that players might not encounter otherwise, deepening the story of the world by encouraging players to explore it fully. Thatgamecompany's 2012 release, *Journey*, for instance, includes little in the way of exposition or explanation. Players begin the game as a hooded figure in red in the middle of a vast desert, and as they travel toward a mountain in the distance, they discover ruins of a civilization. Throughout the game, players explore these ruins, learning game mechanics such as jumping and gliding and interacting with features of the environment to solve puzzles. The landscape of *Journey* is beautiful and artistic, full of fascinating structures and playful mechanics, such as flying and sliding. Many levels end with an interaction with a white-robed ancestor, and a "vision," which helps to provide some context for what has happened to the ruined civilization.

In the article "Game Movement as Enactive Focalization," Yotam Shibolet discusses Mieke Bal's work applying Gérard Genette's concept of narrative focalization to visual media forms, arguing that the kinesthetic experience of navigating the world of *Journey*, helps to mimic bodily experience with the potential to create a physical link between the player and the game narrative. Shibolet writes, "enactive focalization could allow us to ask how various aspects of movement dynamics design affect instantiated player experience ... Researching the significance of movement dynamics designed by different games, or utilized differently by different players, could produce valuable theoretical insight for the study of environmental storytelling" (62). In other words, beyond rewarding exploration with improved story events, or a more developed understanding of the world, environmental storytelling has the potential to create a physical link between player and narrative whether by mimicking realistic movement, or, as in *Journey*, creating an entirely new sensation of moving through a world, a premise that offers fascinating implications for narrative experience through environmental storytelling.

The game rewards exploring the world in-depth by featuring symbols, which can be found in secret locations and increase a player's abilities, and murals, which are visual images hidden throughout the world that can be activated to reveal an element of the world's history. It is possible to complete the game without discovering these artifacts, but exploring the world rewards the player with a deeper understanding of the world and its history, through visual images that players must interpret on their own. The world of *Journey* is mysterious, complex, and intriguing, and it is up to players to piece together much of the story of its history through exploration and examination. In this way, the central embedded story of the game – the player's journey to the mountain – is augmented by the emergent story of the landscape, which players traverse as they see fit, choosing the extent to which they are interested in learning more about the history of the world. In this way, environmental storytelling works alongside mechanics such as meaningful choice, character development, and failure and replay, asking players to be active agents in uncovering and piecing together the narrative. Beyond being simply a setting for events, a digital game environment is a crucial vector for storytelling, one that rewards exploration and scrutiny, thereby forging deep emotional bonds – and possibly, as Shibolet suggests, even bodily memories – that foster a close connection to and investment in the narrative.

Journey is also an excellent example of a further element that game-based storytelling offers, namely, social connection and interaction. The story of the world and its ruins is told visually throughout the game, which includes little in the way of words or dialogue. If players elect to play the game in online mode, however, they may encounter another player, another hooded figure also traversing the same levels and engaging with the same environment. Other than an electronic chirping sound and a visual symbol to indicate the player has pushed the button to make it, there is no way to communicate with the other players that one encounters. Players may choose to charge one another's scarves, which makes certain game mechanics easier, or they can explore together, or ignore one another entirely. At the end of the game, the credits list of usernames of the other players that one has encountered on the journey, but until that time, players have no access to any information about the other person accompanying them. Shibolet notes the ways that this multiplayer dynamic encourages kinesthetic connection with the game, arguing that:

> In the absence of affordances for lingual expression, [players] attempt communication through abstract movements ... This can allow the players to enact all sorts of minimalistic visual and musical performances for each other, or together. Thereby, Journey's movement design can instantiate fluid and abstract experiential narratives of bonding with another purely through shared travel. (64)

Shibolet contends that the lack of lingual communication serves to amplify and encourage the physical experience of the game, highlighting the ways that even simple multiplayer social elements such as this one can shape the experience of a game narrative in compelling ways.

In an interview with *Eurogamer*, Jenova Chen, the creative director for the game, explains the goals for the multiplayer elements of *Journey*, saying, "We want people to trust, befriend, fall in love and rely on each other in this game," though ultimately the easiest way to encourage these connections was to limit the interactions that players could have, leading to a "single-player game that you can simply experience with another player" (Cullen). According to Kellee Santiago, the studio head for *Journey*, even with stripped-down mechanics, "'It just feels different ... Even when you take away nearly every game mechanic you can to validate having another person there. It still feels different to have another person there" (Cullen). Robin Hunicke, a producer for Thatgamecompany says, "We really wanted *Journey* to feel like a place ... Like a place you visit, a relic, like a ruin. Like if you go see the Parthenon or something like that, we wanted it to feel like *that*. Like there [were] ghosts in there and there was a sense of respect and wonder and mystery about just being there" (Cullen). Often celebrated for the uniqueness of the social interactions within the game, *Journey* illustrates the ways that experiencing a narrative with another person, even without the capacity to speak to them directly, can have a profound impact on the experience of a story. In the book *How Games Move Us: Emotion by Design*, Katherine Isbister writes:

> Journey's designers use avatar visual design and physical responsiveness, vast and majestic landscapes and soundscapes, and powerful minimalist tools for coordinated action and communication to create a dramatic and transformative experience for players. Emotionally, playing the game evokes the sort of feelings that come up when sharing a challenging but temporary real-world adventure with someone. (122)

Sharing unique moments within a game creates an emotional connection between players, bonding them in a way that heightens and amplifies the events of the story. This effectively changes the narrative experience from an expected story, one that all players experience in the same way, into something individual, unique, and memorable, a narrative with the potential to be markedly different each time a player engages with it.

In his book *Convergence Culture: Where Old and New Media Collide,* Henry Jenkins discusses the ways that entertainment experiences in contemporary society are increasingly social in nature. Jenkins notes the ways that the boundaries between media producer and consumer are often blurred, as social media and internet culture enable people to find platforms for their creative work and ideas without the support of the traditional gatekeepers such publishers and media companies. Consumers feel empowered to engage with creative works, whether it is by writing fan fiction stories based on their favorite television series, by working with others to uncover spoilers for reality television, or by interacting with transmedia storytelling experiences that encourage participants to shape the narrative by engaging with the characters on social media or by solving puzzles with other viewers. Contemporary storytelling experiences are increasingly collective and multimodal, and video game narratives are no exception. Whether players are experiencing a story together in-game as with *Journey*; are sharing experiences and knowledge collectively through online forums or social media platforms like Discord; or are playing for an audience or watching other gamers play on an online streaming platform such as Twitch, digital game narratives are frequently experienced in connection with others. Because of the predominance of social interaction in digital gaming spaces and the potential for shared elements to have a dramatic impact on the experience of a story, analyses of digital game narratives are incomplete without an examination of collaborative features, which are crucial elements of video game storytelling.

Jenkins notes a shift to collective intelligence, whether that involves managing the complex lineages and histories of the houses in George R. R. Martin's *Game of Thrones* series, piecing together observations in order to predict what happens in a season of the reality show *Survivor*, or solving the puzzles in a transmedia narrative such as *The Beast*, which was released in connection with Steven Spielberg's film *A.I.: Artificial Intelligence*, contemporary audiences are increasingly accustomed to experiencing stories with others as well as taking an active role in the narrative. Jenkins explains that "collective intelligence refers to this ability of virtual communities to leverage the combined expertise of their members. What we cannot know or do on our own, we may now be able to do collectively" (27). In essence, collaborative experience may feel increasingly vital to contemporary narrative, in the sense that a story experienced alone is relatively incomplete, or somehow insufficient. From the perspective of digital games, collaboration is important in that players may need to work together to keep track of the vast and complicated histories of complex digital worlds. They may create resources to share important information. In *Journey*, for instance, players might turn to playthrough videos or online forums for help locating murals or hidden symbols, while in *Life Is Strange*, players may look for help when faced with certain choices, or they may note the in-game mechanism at the end of each chapter, which gives a percentage comparison between the choices an individual player has made with those made by other players. Even in *Journey*, where players may simply be traversing a level with a nameless stranger, leading them across sand dunes or experimenting with the mechanics afforded by a machine half-buried in the ruins, the collective experience of mystery and wonder is a powerful force, one that changes the story, making it unique and tailored. It imparts a game experience with the sublime, the sense that each particular playthrough is one-of-a-kind, created through the interplay of unique social elements that would be impossible to replicate or re-create even if a player wanted to do so.

The collective and collaborative elements of video games are particularly interesting when considered in tandem with the concept of procedural rhetoric, or the idea that games often require players to participate in systems that perpetuate a particular worldview and ideology. Ian Bogost discusses this concept in depth in his 2007 book, *Persuasive Games: The Expressive Power of Videogames*. Bogost explains that because games are often dismissed as escapist entertainment, their rhetorical capacity is rarely considered by contemporary audiences, who may be particularly vulnerable to these persuasive mechanisms. Bogost provides the example of the Molleindustria game, *The McDonald's Videogame*, which was released in 2006. This free-to-play game is not endorsed by the McDonald's company and instead offers a biting critique of the fast-food industry, giving players the option to make ethically questionable choices such as supporting child advertising, underpaying employees, and feeding cattle contaminants and additives. To win at the game, players must engage in unethical behavior, which makes *The McDonald's Videogame* such an effective critique. Bogost argues that whereas in other media, audiences might learn about these practices passively, by reading about them in a book or viewing information about them in a documentary, in the digital game, players are forced to participate in this system. This enables players to see firsthand how a company might be inclined to make such dubious choices, particularly when expected to make decisions quickly amid financial pressures. In Bogost's view, by asking players to actively participate, games act as particularly compelling persuasive media.

In the case of *The McDonald's Videogame*, the ideological goals of the game are overt and clear, but Bogost makes the case that all games act as mechanisms of ideology on some level, whether their creators intend it or not. In his article "The Rhetoric of Video Games," published in the anthology *The Ecology of Games: Connecting Youth, Games, and Learning*, Bogost argues:

> Video games are models of real and imagined systems. We always play when we use video games, but the sort of play that we perform is not always the stuff of leisure. Rather, when we play, we explore the possibility space of a set of rules – we learn to understand and evaluate a game's meaning. Video games make arguments about how social or cultural systems work in the world – or how they could work, or don't work ... When we play video games, we can interpret these arguments and consider their place in our lives. (136)

As entertainment experiences, Bogost argues that games are particularly powerful persuasive mechanisms, even more so because players often do not consider the ideological mechanisms at work. In "The Rhetoric of Video Games," Bogost argues that educators and parents must take an active role in helping young people to identify these processes, much in the same way that they are taught to identify the persuasive powers of advertising. Critics of the concept of proceduralism question the extent to which a game's rules and mechanics determine its meaning, arguing that play, by nature, is complex, emergent and difficult to predict. In "Against Procedurality," Miguel Sicart argues that player behavior is more central to establishing a game's meaning than a game's rules and systems.

Sicart argues that by emphasizing the extent to which the designer-encoded rules of a game determine its meaning, theorists have overlooked a crucial component of games, namely, the extent to which players themselves bring meaning to a game by the ways they engage with it. Sicart writes:

> What proceduralists deny is the capacity for players to affect the game with their virtues, to explore their relation with what the game proposes by means of their values and political ideas. Players are creative, engaged, value-driven agents who engage in play with their own values as part of what helps them configure their experience.

Like Bell and Ensslin, Sicart advocates for an empirical examination of games, which prioritizes collecting and examining responses of players rather than a formalist approach, prioritizing the meaning inherent in a game's rules and processes.

Regardless of where theorists fall on the spectrum of centering a game's meaning on player behavior or attributing it to the rules and systems inherent in a game's code, conversations about the values inherent in game design are increasingly common among designers. In the book *Values at Play in Digital Games*, Mary Flanagan and Helen Nissenbaum argue that game developers should include value design as an overt element of the game design process. Flanagan and Nissenbaum argue that "system design is typically guided by goals such as reliability, efficiency, resilience, modularity, performance, safety, and cost. We suggest adding items like fairness, equality, and sustainability to the list" (9). Claims such as these are similar to those made by Stephen Knight in *Form and Ideology in Crime Fiction*, where he explores the social functions of crime narratives, noting that each work "has a special, formal way of presenting the world to us" (5). Knight examines the ways that classic mystery authors across time periods and geographical locales – Edgar Allan Poe, Agatha Christie, Raymond Chandler, and others – use the conventions of the mystery genre to comment on and explore pressing concerns of the time. Similarly, proceduralists, like Bogost, argue that the conventions of game design operate as ideological systems, compelling players to act within conceptual frameworks of which they are unaware. When applied to digital crime narratives, proceduralists invite us to consider what happens when players are asked to actively engage in methods of investigation. How might digital games encourage audiences to think more critically about the role that complex systems such as politics, incarceration, race, and class play in crime narratives, and to what extent might these experiences encourage players to look more closely at their own role within these systems in their day to day lives?

Throughout the remainder of this article, I will illustrate how the fundamental game design and game studies concepts explained earlier can be used to explore the unique mechanisms that digital games offer in telling mystery stories. Although it may be tempting to engage with digital games solely from the perspective of narrative studies, applying literary critical frameworks without a consideration of the unique affordances and effects offered by digital games ignores a significant element of game experiences. Whether considering the distinct influence of the magic circle, the responsibility and agency afforded by elements like failure, meaningful choice, and environmental storytelling, or the potential for social elements to influence a game's impact, it is evident that digital games offer narrative experiences that are difficult to replicate in other forms of media. Further, as audiences become accustomed to these important digital storytelling mechanisms, it is likely that these strategies will become increasingly prevalent in more traditional print forms as well, particularly within the crime genre, which, as I have noted earlier, foregrounds reader participation.

As mechanisms for telling stories, digital games offer diverse and complex opportunities for interactivity and participation, often with the potential to represent systemic issues in contemporary society or impact real-world change. At the end of his book *Persuasive Games*, Bogost issues a call to readers to consider the ways in which games act as important artifacts, encouraging players to reflect on social, political, and cultural systems and to consider their place within them. He writes, "We must recognize the persuasive and expressive power of procedurality ... As players of videogames and other computational artifacts, we should recognize procedural rhetoric as a new way to interrogate our world, to comment on it, to disrupt and challenge it" (340). Bogost's work centers the idea that games are not simply artifacts for entertainment but are powerful mechanisms for shaping culture and perspective. Though Bogost is skeptical of the capacity for digital games to tell effective stories, he believes that games hold a great deal of power within contemporary culture to shape audience viewpoints and perspectives. He writes, "Despite the computers that host them, despite the futuristic and mechanical fictional worlds they often render, videogames are not expressions of the machine. They are expressions of being human. And the logics that drive our games make claims about who we are, how our world functions, and what we want it to become" (340).

It may be tempting to see the scholarship of digital crime narratives as an extension of existing literary explorations, broadening the scope of the field and the canon to allow a space for contemporary forms of storytelling. Instead, we should consider the ways that examinations of digital games can expand our vocabulary for identifying, discussing, and investigating our conceptions of what crime narratives are and how they work, regardless of media form. The games industry is a lucrative, popular social force, and stories told in this medium – consider, for instance, *The Last of Us*, *The Witcher*, and *The Legend of Zelda: Breath of the Wild* – are often well-known cultural touchstones beloved by millions. Rather than viewing video game scholarship as an opening of the field to provide a space for these narratives, we should instead consider the possibility that these widespread, contemporary digital experiences are altering what it means to experience a story, or to tell one, in a way that has profound implications for the future of narrative studies across all media forms.

Environmental Storytelling and Empathy in *Gone Home* and *Firewatch*

In the next section, I will look closely at a variety of digital mystery narratives and explore the ways that the game studies concepts described earlier can augment and enhance the impact of the story. Each game may not include all elements I have described, or those elements may not all be particularly insightful or relevant in each instance, but I have done my best to choose examples that illustrate the wide and varied ways that game design mechanisms can work together to influence a story. First, I will focus on two strong examples of mystery narratives told through environmental storytelling: The Fullbright Company's 2013 release, *Gone Home*, and Campo Santo's 2016 title, *Firewatch*.

Firewatch and *Gone Home* are both compelling narrative-centered games based around the core central mechanic of first-person exploration. Often called "walking simulators" (sometimes derogatorily), games like *Firewatch* and *Gone Home* prioritize enabling players to examine an environment, slowly piecing together a story through observation and discovery. In the article "Why Are We So Afraid to Walk?," published in *Kill Screen,* Miguel Penabella notes the ways that first-person walking games "are often charged as being 'not games' or failing to adhere to familiar means of expression," generally because the term "game" is often associated with an experience that is much more fast-paced and action-oriented. Melissa Kagan's 2022 book, *Wandering Games*, dedicated to critical examinations of walking simulators, contends that games in this genre occupy a unique capacity as "games that are interested in alternative modes of expression, embodiment, environment, orientation, and community" (2). Kagan contends that these kinds of games build upon a long heritage of "walking in fiction, philosophy, pilgrimage, performance, and protest" (2), with the potential to offer revolutionary re-imaginings that "show us different ways of relating toward gender, colonialism, work, and death ... [to] help us imagine what it would be – what it might take – to walk our way into a different sort of world" (28).

Though debates about what is and is not a game are beyond the scope of this Element, it's worth noting the central role that walking simulators occupy in these debates, and Kagan's and Penabella's claims about the impacts of this kind of game are a worthwhile starting point for considering the benefits of environmental storytelling. Penabella explains that first-person walkers:

> usually demand more from players, asking them to consider the worth of environmental storytelling and embedded narratives by calling attention to their input via walking and looking ... We walk and we look through a single perspective, whether that be a flesh-and-blood character or something more ethereal and nonphysical, a consciousness or a temperament. First-person walkers employ movement within an environment to convey moods and ideas more crucially than other kinds of games, encouraging a contemplative, participatory mindset over guided directness. Decelerating action underlines what videogames can do at its most basic level – movement and sight – [contributing to] a deeper entrance towards sensations and experiences often overlooked.

Penabella highlights the ways that telling a story through observation and exploration places a great deal of responsibility on players to engage with the world, affording a strong sense of ownership of the narrative, even if, as is arguably the case with both examples, players have limited influence over the actual events of the story. Even without significant instances of meaningful choice, however, *Gone Home* and *Firewatch* act as excellent examples of the ways that environmental exploration can foster agency within a narrative in important ways.

Gone Home is particularly interesting in the ways that it uses environmental exploration and world construction to emphasize important elements of the mystery and to add to the story's central tension. Players explore *Gone Home* as Katie Greenbriar, a twenty-two-year-old who returns late at night, during a thunderstorm, from a lengthy trip abroad. Katie arrives at the home her parents and younger sister have moved to in her absence – an old mansion left to her father Terry by his Uncle Oscar – to find the house deserted, and players move through the house, rummaging through rooms, drawers, and cupboards, to try and determine what has happened to Katie's family, primarily her sister, Sam. The story is set in 1995 and is packed with technical artifacts and pop culture details from that time, including a fierce soundtrack of riot grrrl bands, and a series of messages that Sam has left for Katie via cassette tapes that tell the story of what Sam has experienced while Katie was away.

Throughout the game, the lights flicker and thunder crashes outside, and while the abandoned mansion is packed with moments that seem like they might come directly from a horror movie – a bathtub splattered with red hair dye, for instance, or a lightbulb that pops when a player interacts with a homemade cross in a secret passageway – the realist traumas at the center of the game are common and relatable. During Katie's absence, Sam has fallen in love with her female friend Lonnie, and after struggling to express her sexuality in an unsupportive environment, Sam has decided to leave to pursue a life with her. Meanwhile, Katie's mother has considered having an affair with a colleague, but instead she and Terry are away at a weekend-long couples' retreat. A close examination of the artifacts in the house further reveals that Terry was sexually abused as a child by Uncle Oscar, who subsequently left him the mansion in his will. These experiences are difficult and traumatic, but compared with the horrific potential scenarios set up by the mood and atmosphere at the beginning of the game, discovering these truths toward the end of game comes as a relief.

In terms of linear narrative, the storyline of *Gone Home* is relatively simple: a young woman returns home and wonders what has happened to her missing family, and by the end of the game she has solved the mystery. In terms of game design, however, the ways that *Gone Home* chooses to execute its storyline highlights the ways that digital mysteries can use environmental storytelling to great effect. First, although players have relative freedom to explore the rooms they encounter, and though they may move freely between rooms in certain sections of the house, the game uses keys and puzzles to ensure that players must examine artifacts carefully, linking the deepening story of what has happened to the characters to specific rooms and sections of the house. In the early rooms of the house, players learn of Sam's developing friendship with Lonnie, which grows into romance as players move upstairs and explore Sam's bedroom. In a blog post entitled "Retrospect Analysis: Gone Home," written by the player Arieces in 2013, Arieces notes the ways that story and plot are closely linked to location, so that events of the story match the tone of the physical location that players are exploring. Arieces describes their experience playing the game saying,

> Consider that "the first kiss" is a high moment and then ... you have to go down into the basement. The game [does] very well at matching the tone of the narrative to the tone of the game ... to derive emotion and reaction from both at the same time. "They kissed, happiness! Oh my god, I have to go into the basement?" And then when you get there, the first sad note appears. Lonnie is leaving. They saved the basement dread for that point in the narrative.

Arieces' description illustrates the ways that *Gone Home*'s environmental game design works from a player's perspective. The game not only uses the emotional associations that players bring to the game (anxiety about descending into a basement, for instance) to heighten tension and increase player engagement, but the narrative further harnesses common fears, using environmental exploration to amplify the emotional experience of the plot.

Most notable from this perspective is the way that the game uses map design to amplify tension and highlight thematic complexities in the narrative. After the initial exposition, players move to the second floor of the house, where they begin exploring Sam's room and learning about her developing feelings for Lonnie. At this point, players encounter a hatch in the ceiling that leads to the attic, which is circled with ominous red holiday lights. They are unable to open the hatch until the end of the game, but it is clear even early in the game that this room holds something important. In Merritt Kopas' "On Gone Home," essay in the *Queer Game Studies* collection edited by Bonnie Ruberg and Adrienne Shaw, Kopas writes,

> Because it's a video game about a big empty house and because it's a story about girls in love, anyone who has any familiarity with either of those genres is going in expecting the worst to happen. Because setting a lesbian love story in a creepy old mansion is the perfect confluence of the terrible. So from the start you're thinking, okay, ghosts. Or suicide. Or probably both. (146)

In the book *Video Games Have Always Been Queer*, Bonnie Ruberg further examines the sadness that Gone Home evokes in many of its players. Ruberg argues that this emotional response "should not be dismissed as merely personal. Sadness is woven into the fabric of the game itself; it is shared by many LGBTQ subjects and relates to systemic social issues and oppression" (173). The red lights around the attic entrance serve as a physical embodiment of the broader social anxieties and trauma that the game's narrative design draws upon, literally looming over the entire house as players progress through the rooms and try to learn what has happened to Sam.

Similarly, when players move to the basement, Arieces notes the correspondence in tone between physical location and the events of the story. Even more importantly though, exploration of the basement leads players to learn more about Oscar, and this is also where players are able to piece together the story about Terry's sexual assault. Details about what has happened to Terry require vigilance and can be easy to miss, but the final clues are located in a narrow hallway in the basement, which leads to a small dark room with a broken light and a toy horse on the floor. Exploration of this room corresponds with one of the darkest revelations in the narrative, and it is also the physical site of Terry's assault, meaning that players learn about his trauma while exploring that space, likely dealing with their own fear and anxiety evoked by the stark details of the environment. Further, this basement room is logistically almost directly below the red lights of the attic, which guard the truth of what happened to Sam.

When I first played *Gone Home*, I was so terrified that I couldn't bring myself to go into the dark room at the end of the hallway, and I resigned myself to missing whatever discoveries were in that room. From a narrative perspective, though, such an impact is profound, and it highlights the power of environmental storytelling. Not only do players learn about the trauma by exploring the place where it happened, but its location in the basement, at the root of the house, illustrates the ways that such traumas tend to hide in the dark recesses of family histories, unspoken, their impacts spiraling out across generations. In the classic work, *Experience: Trauma, Narrative, and History*, Cathy Caruth argues that trauma is not only "the story of the individual in relation to the events of his own past, but as the story of the way in which one's own trauma is tied up with the trauma of another, the way in which trauma may lead ... to the very possibility and surprise of listening to another's wound" (7), an experience which may be traumatizing in itself. I couldn't bring myself to enter that room much in the same way that the family couldn't bring itself to engage with Terry's trauma, and in that moment, I unconsciously enacted that family pattern, feeling it emotionally, while actively participating in it. Further, the placement of that room, deep in the house, beneath the red lights of the attic, helps to explain the lack of connection and support plaguing the family, a physical representation of the reasons why Sam must leave the house to grow into her own identity.

In a 2013 interview with Jeremy Peel for *PC Gamer*, *Gone Home* developer Steve Gaynor talks about some of the design choices at work in the game. Most interestingly, Gaynor describes the responsibility the game puts on the player to piece together the story. When designing the game, the team asked themselves:

> How are we going to allow the player to fully, interactively inhabit a role in this immersive space that is non-linear? ... If you find all the pieces [of Sam's story], it's told to you. And then for everything else [it's] along a spectrum ... The further away that core story is, chronologically or character-wise, the more work the player has to do to add it up and put it together themselves ... The story of the game is essentially like a puzzle that you're putting together.

Gaynor's comments unconsciously mirror Turchi's ideas about mystery narratives in *A Muse and A Maze*, and the role Turchi ascribes to mystery writers as puzzle creators, leading readers down a careful revelation of revelations and surprises. Gaynor's team similarly considers themselves to be constructing a puzzle, albeit one where players hold primary responsibility for uncovering the clues and piecing together the details of the story. By relying on horror tropes, the game encourages players to imbue the game with a certain emotional weight and expectation, one that transfers to the events of the story, and by asking players to take on the role of Katie, they are encouraging the audience to approach the story as a family member, someone who is invested in the events and in learning about the truth. The use of horror is intended to draw audiences in enough to develop interest in the characters. Gaynor explains, "By the back half of the game you're no longer playing because you want to find out when the horror thing is finally going to happen ... but because you're actually invested in the characters and their story for the people that they are."

The choice to use horror tropes to draw audiences into a narrative where the central revelation is lesbian sexuality is ethically questionable, but even so, *Gone Home* is widely recognized for being one of the first mainstream titles to tell this kind of story, and for many players with similar experiences, seeing characters like themselves in a widely celebrated video game remains a moving and impactful experience. Ruberg writes that "little critical attention has been paid to the feelings of sadness that *Gone Home* stirs in its players. In my discussions with other queer players, many have reported crying while playing the game. These tears are evidence of the game's ability to connect with players whose own difficult personal histories mirror those represented on-screen" (173). By placing the responsibility for uncovering the story in the hands of the players, the game uses environmental storytelling to develop connection and empathy between the story's characters and the audience, and by asking players to enter the game through the lens of Katie's character, they further ensure that players will approach the game from a position of empathy, even if the subject matter makes players uncomfortable or if they have little experience with it themselves.

Within the magic circle of the game, players feel agency and responsibility for unraveling the story and solving the mystery, as well as a sense of safety that encourages them to sit with perspectives that might be different from their own. Sam isn't their own sister, but she is Katie's, and Katie's character, arguably the least developed in the game, is nebulous enough for players to identify with her desire to learn the fate of her family. Kopas describes her experience with *Gone Home* as a queer player, writing, "Katie isn't so much a character in *Gone Home*. She's the camera. And for someone like me who never really felt present as a kid, who always felt like she was observing other people and never really observing herself – her own feelings, her own body – that's kind of perfect" (148). *Gone Home* uses environmental storytelling to encourage players to solve a mystery, but the hidden elements within the narrative aren't only the story of what has happened to Katie's family. Game design elements work in tandem with the narrative to further speak to experiences that have often been kept hidden, whether those are family traumas, social and cultural systems that often discriminate against LGBTQ+ experience, or the difficult work that many queer people must do to uncover and live their own identities in a world that seems intent on silencing them.

The capacity for digital mystery narratives to encourage empathy among players through environmental storytelling, often in ways that offer the potential for profound real-life impact, is also effective in the game *Firewatch*, a first-person walking exploration game that asks players to take on the role of Henry, who has recently started a job as a fire lookout in a remote state park in the Wyoming wilderness. Unlike *Gone Home*, where players learn a great deal of information about Katie's family while uncovering relatively minimal information about her own character, *Firewatch* encourages audiences to connect closely to Henry's character, despite his complicated past and flawed nature. The game begins with a text-based character creation segment, where players learn about Henry's relationship with his wife Julia and make choices about his past behavior. For instance, when Julia comes home late, does Henry get mad, or does he ignore her? As time progresses, Julia develops early onset dementia, and players must make choices on Henry's behalf. Does he move her into a care facility? Does he try to care for her himself? Eventually Julia's parents take her home to Australia to live with them, and the game begins with Henry hiking to the lookout tower at his new job. Whatever choices a player makes in the beginning, Henry begins the game with a complicated past with difficult decisions. He's an imperfect character with a complex past, like many people, and as the player has made choices on his behalf, they are imperfect alongside him. Barely ten minutes into the game, and players have already had a meaningful impact on Henry's character over the course of many years of his life, and so when he arrives at his tower in the wilderness and strange things begin happening, they are invested not just in the mysteries of the story, but also in helping Henry navigate them.

Much as in *Gone Home*, the central storyline of Firewatch follows a relatively embedded structure, and though gameplay is emergent to the extent that players have a great deal of freedom in exploring the wilderness around Henry's tower and are given some opportunity for meaningful choice in developing his character, the story's events unfold the same way in each playthrough.

Initially, Henry is tasked with relatively mundane tasks typical of a park ranger. He must investigate illegal use of fireworks, pick up discarded beer cans, argue with skinny-dipping teens, gather supplies, and examine the remains of a sliced communication wire. As Henry completes these tasks, however, he's pulled into a deeper mystery that ultimately makes him question the world around him. His tower is broken into, his windows smashed, and while investigating the teens supposedly responsible for this vandalism, Henry uncovers a strange encampment with notes that suggest that he and his fellow lookout, Delilah, are under surveillance. While hiking through the wildness, trying to understand what is going on, Henry learns more about Ned, a Vietnam veteran struggling with PTSD who worked as a lookout with his son, Brian, before disappearing. Henry finds Brian's comic books and secret hideout, before eventually finding Brian's corpse, the victim of an apparent climbing accident. Fires rage in the wilderness, and just before he must evacuate, Henry finds evidence that Ned has remained in the park the whole time, mourning the death of his son, for which he feels responsible, and fabricating the materials to make it seem as though Henry and Delilah are under surveillance.

The events of the story remain relatively consistent across playthroughs, though, as in *Gone Home*, players have a great deal of agency in examining artifacts, reading letters, and learning more about the world. Interactivity in *Firewatch* comes primarily through Henry's relationship with Delilah, whom Henry talks to entirely via walky-talky. As a senior firewatch, Delilah advises Henry on what to do, and as he travels through the park, the two communicate regularly, developing a humorous relationship and easy camaraderie. Players choose Henry's responses to Delilah, and even have the option to ignore her entirely, though the relationship eventually develops romantic overtones. Players are also able to choose Henry's responses to what happens to him. Does he set fire to the teenagers' camp? Does he tell Delilah the truth about his actions? In this way, meaningful choice in *Firewatch* is largely centered on character and relationship development. As in the opening narrative, Henry's responses are complex and human. He is funny, and clearly struggling to navigate his past with Julia and his developing friendship with Delilah, while also making sense of the strange events around him. In a 2016 review of the game written for *The Guardian*, Nathan Ditum explains the extent to which the game succeeds in creating empathy for Henry. He writes:

> Everything that happens to Henry in the park is designed to highlight his vulnerabilities. With his life paused and broken, his increasing dependence on Delilah begins to feel like an emotional precipice, the skewed power dynamic and his fragility a tinderbox mix. Meanwhile, the park itself envelopes him physically, this stocky, everyday nobody tumbling through the oblivious vastness of this wild place. And it works. Which is to say that we care, and that Henry feels like us.

In *Firewatch*, the choices and characters are flawed and complicated, and it is impossible to play Henry perfectly. Giving players the responsibility for his choices and asking them to navigate the forest on his behalf helps to create empathy for Henry, and whether players agree with Henry or even like him, they feel connected to him, invested in his experiences and accountable for his actions.

Like *Gone Home*, *Firewatch* uses design techniques that encourage players to connect with characters and behaviors that may be quite unlike their own, and to empathize with Henry rather than judge his actions. Although the game features an occasional soundtrack, players spend most of the game wandering in nature in relative silence, exploring a scenic and realistically rendered wilderness that is, at times, just as confusing to navigate as a real-world counterpart. This slow-paced hiking encourages players to reflect, offering ample time to think about the events and the characters, a technique that helps to encourage empathy.

As in *Gone Home*, players learn about other characters primarily by engaging with their artifacts, and the more they explore, the more they are rewarded with story details. Whether they are learning about Brian's fear of climbing or piecing together the story of a gay love affair between two former rangers by examining notes left in cache boxes, players are encouraged to engage with the environment and put together the story for themselves, a process that creates a sense of responsibility for the narrative and its characters even if players don't necessarily identify with their choices. By feeling accountable for Henry's actions, players are more likely to sympathize with his situation and to empathize with the emotional connection he feels with Delilah, even if they feel critical of his emotional infidelity. Similarly, using environmental storytelling to encourage players to learn more about Ned while investigating his camp slows the pace of the revelations of his character, giving players a sense of agency while also affording them time to consider his postwar PTSD and the impact it might have had on his parenting experiences with Brian. Even if players deeply disapprove of his choices, particularly in the way he handled Brian's death, it is likely they also understand his anger, paranoia, and grief, and consequently the reasons he acted in the ways he did. *Firewatch* is full of complicated characters, all of whom are clearly struggling with past choices and traumas, and the game design choices help to encourage connection and understanding.

Not only are the characters in *Firewatch* complicated and difficult to classify, but the mystery, too, is unsatisfying in its solutions. Brian is dead, and Ned is wrestling with his culpability, but to what extent is Ned responsible, and to what degree are his responses a by-product of his war trauma? Delilah claims to have no knowledge of Ned's activities, but there are numerous indications that she and Ned were close, possibly even romantically involved, and that perhaps she was even involved in the attempts to fool Henry into believing there was a broader plot of surveillance. There are larger questions, too, about Henry's place in the story. Was Ned trying to dissuade Henry from finding Brian's body, or did he ultimately want Henry to uncover what happened? To what extent did Delilah know the truth? Was she aware of Ned's hideout? Is she still involved with Ned? Given these questions, how should we interpret her romantic connection with Henry? At the end of the game, Henry hikes toward the evacuation point at Delilah's tower with the promise of finally meeting her in-person, only to have her tell him that she's decided to leave on an earlier flight. She encourages Henry to go back to his wife, and players must either navigate Henry onto an evacuation helicopter or allow the game to end with Henry refusing to evacuate and being lost to the fire.

Using a game to tell *Firewatch*'s story emphasizes the complexity of the characters and narrative. The more time players spend exploring the forest and learning about its inhabitants, the more keenly we feel the absence of true answers. Perhaps if we spent more time wandering, or if we selected different responses to Delilah, or if we looked even more closely at the artifacts we discover, we would finally be able to learn the truth of what has happened, of who these characters are and why they act the ways they do. Such agency and capability, though, is an illusion, much the way it is in real life. People are confusing and complicated, often acting in ways they do not understand themselves, and there are many mysteries that evade clear solutions, leading instead to more questions. Even if players restart the game, intent on making alternate choices or approaching the story differently, they will still fail at uncovering the story, because a complete answer to these questions can never be fully known.

In *A Muse & A Maze*, Turchi differentiates between the puzzles and mysteries of crime narratives, explaining that such narratives often work as breadcrumbs, leading readers down a trail of questions in which they are able to uncover the truth of what has happened, who has committed a crime, and how, and why. Turchi contrasts such puzzles with the "state of wonder or contemplation" of "true, unsolvable mysteries" (57), the universal questions of existence, which draw readers to fiction, hoping to find answers or insights into the unknowable elements of human existence. *Firewatch* features a puzzle that reveals the true mysteriousness at the heart of many crime narratives, even after the specifics have been uncovered. What has happened here and why? How will it shape Henry, and what does it mean for the other characters? And beyond these specific questions about setting and character, the piece alludes to larger questions that are central to human existence. How do we move forward in the face of trauma? Given the confusing and confounding difficulties of life, how is it possible to connect to others, or indeed, to ever fully know them? Is it even possible to fully understand ourselves? Ditum argues that "*Firewatch* is about solitude and space, a first-person journey through the massive wilderness of American's Shoshone National Forest. It's a space of such magnitude that it almost unavoidably conjures mysteries and conspiracies of corresponding size. But in this game, we are drawn back down to the essential and human." *Firewatch* may take place in a vast wilderness, but in the end, it is a story about the wilderness inside us all. The game design elements allow Campo Santo to center players in the mystery, encouraging them to try again in the face of uncertainty even if they will ultimately fail. In this way, the piece forces players to inhabit the same emotional space as its characters, trying and failing repeatedly to know the unknowable, a complex narrative experience that would be difficult to replicate in any other medium.

As an approach to mystery narratives, environmental storytelling allows creators to give players a central place in the story, asking them to take on the role of an investigator, essentially making them responsible for uncovering the clues and deciphering them. This process invariably creates a close connection between the player and the world of the story, as they must learn about a space in detail, traversing and exploring, looking closely at what has been left behind in order to understand what has happened there. Whether on behalf of an underdeveloped central perspective, like Katie in *Gone Home*, or a deeply complicated character such as Henry in *Firewatch*, environmental exploration holds a great potential for asking players to empathize and connect with a story and its characters, even if the circumstances and experiences are different than their own. It's worth noting, too, the potential for games such as Simogo's 2024 game, *Lorelei and the Laser Eyes*, to go even further, incorporating puzzles that require players to step even more firmly into the technical role of the detective, studying the environment, using their own pen and paper to jot notes and make calculations, and blurring the boundaries between the game world and the real one. Environmental storytelling can be used to emphasize the unknowable, to highlight the mysteries of human existence, and to encourage players to sit with difficult and complicated truths. In asking players to explore a space and giving them the freedom to engage with that world deeply, digital games hold a great capacity for involving audiences in complex mysteries and encouraging them to connect with characters and experiences outside their own.

Meaningful Choice, Implication, and Culpability in *Pentiment* and *Disco Elysium*

The environmental storytelling described in *Gone Home* and *Firewatch* is effective in engaging players in the process of piecing together a mystery and giving them a sense of responsibility and agency in exploring closely and examining the things they find. In both games, however, the central storyline is relatively fixed. Players have the opportunity for agency and choice in deciding where to explore and how closely to examine the things they encounter, but while their choices might impact the order they uncover elements, or whether they miss a piece of the story entirely, there is little in the way of meaningful choice to give players the sense of influencing the narrative. As described earlier, integrating meaningful choice into a narrative enables players to shape the story or its characters in an emergent way, allowing players to influence the story and change it in ways that often increase a sense of responsibility and investment. In this section, I will examine the games *Pentiment* and *Disco Elysium* to illuminate the ways that meaningful choice can work together with other game design elements to implicate players in the events of a story. When these techniques are used in crime narratives, this can result in a sense of player culpability, making broader arguments that implicate players and ask them to consider the complex systems of justice in our own world.

Pentiment, which was released by Obsidian Entertainment in 2022, illustrates the ways that digital games can succeed in exploring a variety of subjects and historical settings. Set in sixteenth-century Bavaria, players take on the role of Andreas Maler, a visiting artist who is working in Kiersau Abbey in the small town of Tassing to illuminate religious manuscripts. When a visiting baron is suddenly murdered, and Maler's friend and fellow artist is wrongfully accused, Maler must begin a hasty investigation to uncover the true killer. Players explore small-town Tassing, sharing meals with inhabitants and learning about religion, politics, and culture, while hurrying to uncover the murderer. At the end of Act I, players must accuse someone, and in fitting with the judicial procedures of the time, someone is executed publicly to atone for the crime. Act II takes place seven years later, when Maler returns to find the townsfolk angry about the heavy taxation imposed on them by the Abbey, which is struggling financially. Just before the townspeople revolt, the leader of the revolution is killed, and Maler again finds himself in a position to investigate the murder, which is accompanied by a series of mysterious notes that are similar to ones he found while investigating the crime in Act I. Maler explores the town, eating with the townsfolk and learning of the ways that the events in the first act have influenced the town and the abbey. Eventually, he accuses a second murderer, who flees to a nearby mill, and is killed when angry townsfolk burn it down along with the abbey and its library. Maler, horrified by the loss of manuscripts, runs into the flames to save them and is killed also.

In Act III, which takes place twenty years later, players take on the role of Magdalene Druckeryn, the daughter of Maler's friend Claus, and a printmaker, which is a relatively new technology, perceived as a danger to the church and its ideas. When her father is injured in an attack, Druckeryn is tasked with painting a mural depicting the town's history in the new town hall, and as she speaks with local townspeople, trying to learn more about the town's history, she encounters notes which, unbeknownst to her, are similar to the ones found by Maler during his early investigations. During Druckeryn's investigations, she learns that Maler has not died after all, but has been living as a hermit in the ruins of the abbey. Together, the two discover that the attack on her father and the earlier murders were inspired by the local priest and a reclusive nun, who were afraid of the townsfolk learning the truth of the pagan roots of many of Tassing's Christian traditions. The priest is killed during an attempt to collapse an underground Roman temple, and the game ends with the completion of Druckeryn's town hall mural, focused on subjects chosen by the player, which will pass on the story of the town and its history to future generations.

Pentiment's complex multigenerational story is heavily rooted in historical research, and it provides a detailed and developed overview of a tumultuous social and political climate with which many players will be unfamiliar. Although the main events of the three acts are the same regardless of player action, and the priest and the nun always emerge at the end of the game as the masterminds behind the events of the previous twenty-seven years, meaningful choice plays a large role in the ways that players experience the main events of the game. First, players have the option at the beginning of each act to select key personality and background traits of the main character for that act (either Maler or Druckeryn), which will influence the ways in which that character engages with the details they encounter. Maler can have a background in logic for instance, or a deep knowledge of oration, or experience with the occult, which will influence the ways he interprets information as well as his capacity for speaking with certain characters. Further, time is clearly limited, which has an impact on the player's actions. They can have Maler participate in a variety of experiences, but there is not enough time for him to engage with every activity. Similarly, Maler often uncovers important information while sharing meals with other characters, but he cannot eat with everyone, and players must choose which experiences seem the most useful to the investigation. Further, depending on the dialogue choices players make, they may be able to persuade certain characters to share important information regarding the crime or its suspects (Brother Guy's embezzling, for instance) or to behave in certain ways (to encourage a character to approach a romantic interest, for example), but players are often unaware of the lasting implications these choices will have on the story. Much as in real life, players understand that their choices impact the story, but frequently there is no explicit mechanism in the game to link these decisions to the outcome.

Though individually these moments of meaningful choice may be small, collectively, they add up to a narrative experience that feels dynamic, tailored to individual player input in ways that are impossible to fully understand or predict. The sense of player responsibility in the story is extensive, and because the character that Maler accuses is killed in each act, the stakes similarly feel quite high. Even so, because of the pressures of time, it is impossible for Maler to explore all possibilities and potentials in a single playthrough, and so the accusations he makes are tenuous and underdeveloped, leading to a sense that the investigation is incomplete, with many questions left unanswered. In a March 2023 review of the game for *PC Magazine,* Jason Cohen notes, "*Pentiment* styles itself as a murder mystery. You question people, gather evidence, investigate hunches, and blame someone for the crime. However, the game only sort of cares about the truth. No matter who you peg as the killer, there are no definitive answers. Instead, you must live with the consequences of your actions." Regardless of whom Maler accuses, there is always the sense that the accusation is not completely founded, that Maler's biases and preconceptions, and by extension the player's, have played a fundamental role in the people he has chosen to investigate and accuse. For instance, when I first played through Act II, I spoke extensively with the innkeeper, Hanna Bergeryn, who seemed quite suspicious. She could easily have committed the murder, and her concerns about the impact that the revolt might have on pilgrimage visits, a significant source of her livelihood, seemed like sufficient motivation. But Brother Guy was mean-mean spirited and embezzling money from the abbey, while Hanna was a mother. Her loss seemed like it might have a negative impact on the town, so I accused Guy. The game leaves it up to the player to wrestle with the biases, guilt, and moral implications of their decisions. Whether Hanna is punished for her crime, leaving her husband and child to mourn her, or whether she survives to run a flourishing inn in the next act, history simply continues, leaving the player to discover how their choices have shaped the world as time advances.

From an ideological perspective, *Pentiment* requires its players to participate and collude with a system where justice is clearly biased and flawed. There is no way to conduct a complete investigation, and it is impossible until the final act to understand the full story of what has happened and who is responsible. The consequences of these suboptimal conditions are clear and indisputable. Players must make choices with sobering penalties, and they watch as characters die on-screen because of the decisions they've made. While the world of *Pentiment* is constrained, as all cultural fictions are, a historical narrative that seems separated from our own by tremendous distances of time and geography, in implicating the player, the game makes an argument about justice in our own world, about the extent to which it is possible to investigate crimes objectively, or to punish them fairly. As players, we have made these choices, and so it is impossible to distance ourselves from these flawed systems. To what extent have we let our biases influence our own judgements? In what ways have we jumped to conclusions too rapidly? How have our perspectives and choices had an impact, influencing our communities and social environments, and spiraling outward to affect history overall? The systems of justice in Pentiment are the clear products of the time period, and the forces of religion, politics, and technology are quite different than our own, but in implicating the player, the game makes arguments about culpability, bias, and perspective that are striking and contemporary.

Beyond examining the weaknesses of justice, *Pentiment* further makes an argument about history, and the ways that flawed decisions in the past lead to the realities of the future. By having the game take place over such a large period of time, the impacts of Maler's choices are clear and evident. Characters who were children in Act I have their own children in Act III, and the ways in which Maler has encouraged the characters to pursue their dreams, to approach their beloveds, or to think about their careers, plays out over the years of the game. Rather than being a story about empirical truth, Cohen writes, "the game cares more about stories and our perception of truth. Tassing is a town with a long, winding history. It was founded by Romans, settled by Pagans, and is currently populated by Christians. The passage of time makes the truth hard to discern, and over the game's three acts, you see how the truth changes depending on your perception." Beyond simply representing history and illustrating the ways that choices in the past led to the stories embraced by the present, the game also asks the player to participate overtly in that process in Act III as they help Druckeryn decide what scenes she will paint on the town hall to honor the town's history.

As Druckeryn chooses which moments to illustrate, she must consider the impact of her decisions. What are the consequences of depicting the town's pagan past? Is it worth commemorating a legend, if those stories anger the church, which might result in severe penalties for the citizens? Are people ready to hear tales about the past that might not fit with what they have previously believed? In asking the player to make choices about representing what has happened, and to consider all the ways that historical narratives are shaped by the agendas and perspectives that can be difficult to understand fully, *Pentiment* highlights the ways that individual choices can become collective stories, passed on over time, gradually hardening into the illusion of concrete truth. In *Form and Ideology in Crime Fiction*, Knight argues for the importance of incorporating knowledge of the audiences and social systems of a work's historical context when examining canonical crime narratives. He writes:

> The content of the text, its omissions and selections, is important. Plot itself is a way of ordering events; its outcome distributes triumph and defeat, praise and blame to the characters in a way that accords with the audience's belief in

> dominant cultural values – which themselves interlock with the social structure. So texts create and justify what has come to be called hegemony, the inseparable bundle of political, cultural, and economic sanctions which maintain a particular social system to the advantage of certain members of the whole community. (4)

By allowing players to shape the events of the story as well as to make decisions about crafting the historical artifact that represents it, *Pentiment* foregrounds the forces that Knight describes. Through its treatment of meaningful choice, the game asks players to participate in an ideological experience that questions the capacity for empirical truth. Even in something as seemingly clear-cut as a murder mystery, the game complicates the idea that it is possible to assess fault and responsibility, and that the resulting uncertainties have profound implications throughout history.

Disco Elysium takes a similar approach in its representation of the difficulties inherent in solving a crime, but in this case, the challenges of knowing the "truth," are less wrapped up in the pressures of perspective and history and are more inherent in the unstable nature of the self. Players explore the open world of Revachol through the perspective of Detective Henry DuBois, a middle-aged detective suffering from substance-induced amnesia and struggling with the traumas associated with being left by his fiancé years before. DuBois is tasked with investigating the murder of a man he learns is Colonel Lely Kortenaer, the head of a group of mercenaries sent to break an ongoing strike by a local dockworkers' union. While investigating the murder, DuBois and his partner Kim Kitsuragi, must navigate the conflict between the dockworkers and the mercenaries, while traversing a town still ravaged by a series of political upheavals, engaging with its citizens who are grappling with a variety of complicated and conflicting ideological perspectives and struggling with economic depression. As a place, Revachol is shaped by people and forces still fighting to define what it is and what it values, and amid these conflicting perspectives, DuBois wrestles with his own forgotten past, fighting to recover a sense of self after his difficult experiences, while also unable to revisit his traumas fully enough to engage with them and learn from them. In *Unclaimed Experience: Trauma, Narrative, and History*, Caruth discusses the ways that "post-traumatic stress disorder reflects the direct imposition on the mind of the unavoidable reality of horrific events, the taking over of the mind, psychically and neurobiologically, by an event that it cannot control" (58), a description that clearly defines DuBois' experience throughout the game. Caruth argues "that trauma is not simply an effect of destruction but also, fundamentally, an enigma of survival" (58), and similarly, DuBois longs to remember as well as to forget, a mental space which is arguably not an ideal platform for trying to solve a murder.

The world of *Disco Elysium* is packed with dialogue options and meaningful choices, most of which have the potential to impact the story in important ways. The game has multiple possible endings, as well as several premature endings, where it is possible for DuBois to kill himself either purposefully or inadvertently for example, or to resign from his job or otherwise give up on the investigation entirely. While it is possible for players to influence the events of the story, the most extensive and engaging opportunities for meaningful choice in the game have less to do with players shaping the story and are more concerned with the ways they are able to affect DuBois himself as a character. At the beginning of the game, players shape Dubois' character either by choosing one of three pre-designed archetypes, or by creating their own custom version of him by assigning him traits in the areas of Intellect, Psyche, Physique, and Motorics. Each of these areas further corresponds with a series of six skills, all of which can be leveled up throughout the game based on choices players make. Using substances such as drugs or alcohol in the game, or equipping clothing or items can further impact these the skills, though often benefits are paired with drawbacks. For instance, equipping the Orange Bum Hat will give DuBois an increase in reaction speed while reducing his rhetoric.

The game also includes a Thought Cabinet, where interactions with characters or objects can introduce a thought into DuBois' mind. If players choose to have him investigate that thought, he will engage with it over a period of time before internalizing it, resulting in a potential thought bonus that can be equipped much like an item. For instance, if players choose to internalize the Hobocop mentality, DuBois will be able to collect additional bottles while traveling the world and turn them in for money. If DuBois fails an authority check during an encounter with another group of characters, he has the option to gain the Finger on the Eject Button perspective, which will prompt him to have suicidal thoughts each night. If the player chooses to have DuBois frequently hit objects, he may gain the Anti-Object Task Force thought, which allows him to heal damage by hitting physical elements of the environment. The Thought Cabinet elements often give DuBois benefits which, when combined with his skills, may help him to solve problems in different ways. Rather than more traditional role-playing games where bonuses are attached to a particular weapon or armor, in *Disco Elysium* these abilities are a part of DuBois' mind and perspective, which means that the choices players make shape the ways he views and engages with the events of the story and the people and objects around him. A version of DuBois who believes himself to be a Hobocop or part of an Anti-Object Task Force interacts with the world very differently than a DuBois who does not.

In *Half-Real*, Jesper Juul details the ways that player choice and interactivity work in tandem to create a detailed view of the game world. Juul notes that "like other fictional worlds, the fictional world of a video game is incompletely specified. But where the viewer of a film or the reader of a novel is certain to have seen all the material that presents the fictional world of the story, video games are special in that skill is required to access all parts of the game" (138). In the case of the Thought Cabinet, players are unable to examine all thoughts completely, meaning that the possibility of other perspectives always exists, beyond the player's immediate experience. In this way, multiple versions of the story and its world are possible, and players are always aware of these other renderings, even as they are aware that their own specific game experience is unique, personal, and ephemeral, difficult to replicate.

In the article "'You Won't Even Know Who You Are Anymore': Bakthininan Polyphony and the Challenge to the Ludic Subject in *Disco Elysium*," Daniel Vella and Magdalena Cielecka argue that the game's emphasis on the malleability of DuBois' character serves to push back against authoritative masculine tropes common in noir detective fiction. Vella and Cielecka write, "Disco Elysium invites a reading as a hyperbolic pastiche of [the noir] tradition, presenting us with a protagonist ... who represents not merely a destabilization, but also a complete and total shattering, of the controlled, rational, and authoritative detective figure" (96). Conor Mckeown further maintains that "through an awareness of action as technologies of the posthuman multiverse, [DuBois] is every materially-probable cop simultaneously" (79), arguing that the game's interactive digital format ensures that players are aware of all the ways that DuBois' character might be influenced by choice and randomness in a given playthrough, contributing to a contradictory, posthuman sense of character that is only afforded through "the fundamental systems and logic that the game has been built on" (79). In other words, DuBois is simultaneously the specific character created through a unique individual playthrough, and a conglomeration of all possible characters in all hypothetical playthroughs, resulting in a complex, posthuman approach to character and subjectivity.

In addition to allowing the player to access unique thought perspectives unique to DuBois, many thought cabinet elements are closely aligned with ideological perspectives associated with the various factions and characters in the game, many of which are similar to ideologies in our own world. In a review of the game's *Final Cut* version for *Wired,* Laurence Russell notes the addition of further political visions, which can have DuBois, "agreeing that war crimes are subjective with dejected students grumbling about the hypothetical hypotheticals of authoritarian communism, or contacting the radically moderate Coalition gunship looming over the city in order to ask when, if ever, centrism will achieve something." The game approaches its ideological perspectives with dark humor and satire, which serves to critique perspectives and engage with contemporary viewpoints in a witty and entertaining way. Russell appreciates how the game uses this approach to engage with current social ideologies, explaining that "usually white creators develop alternate-world settings to escape uncomfortable conversations, though in *Disco Elysium* they seem clearer than ever, whether you're indulging them or not. Inescapable at the sharp ends of society, alive and kicking in the game's postcolonial setting." Not only does the game represent a variety of political, social, and historical ideologies, it pokes fun at them equally, using humor to push back against the biases and viewpoints players inevitably bring to the game. Further, because DuBois is able to engage with and adopt these perspectives, most of which offer both drawbacks and benefits, the game highlights how easy it is for people to adopt ideological perspectives; the ways that character perception influences the events of the story; and the likelihood that judicial systems and supposedly "objective" approaches to solving crime are rooted in problematic and convoluted worldviews. Even if the events are the same across playthroughs, it is unlikely that DuBois will be exactly the same from one game to the next, and because player choice impacts everything from the dialogue options available, to the language DuBois uses, to the ways other characters perceive and interact him, each playthrough feels drastically different in meaningful ways.

At its heart, *Disco Elysium* explores the pliability of the human psyche and all of the ways that our experiences shape who we become and how we see the world, whether those things are drugs and alcohol, our past traumas, the ideologies and narratives we invent or buy into to make sense of the world, our jobs and companions, or the things that happen to us. In an interview with Ivy Taylor in 2018, the game's designer and writer Robert Kurvitz describes the role substance abuse plays in the game, and the team's goal of representing complex psychological states marked by loss and pain. Kurvitz tells Taylor:

> The actual ravages that [people] meet are economic, personal . . . The wearing away of dreams, slowing [*sic*] succumbing to alcoholism and mostly just heartbreak and disappointment in human beings . . . It's also quite possible to be mourning the passing of someone who is still living, which is what literally every one of us has [done] at some point in life. Some things end and we just don't want them to. But people make decisions, they leave each other's side. Friends will leave you, lovers will leave you . . . They leave behind a giant fucking mess of shit in your head . . . and just diminished faith in humanity.

Like the characters in *Pentiment*, DuBois is a person shaped by what has happened to him, and by the ways that he has chosen to internalize or engage with the perspectives of the specific place and time where he lives. In *Disco Elysium*, though, players must engage with these conflicting ideologies without the safety of the detached, observer perspective afforded to Maler and Druckeryn. Regardless of the choices players make, DuBois' psyche is constantly altered by the things he experiences, and the world of the game changes, persistently and dynamically along with it.

Whereas *Pentiment* raises epistemological questions about truth, and the ways that individual choices lead to historical narratives that may mask important perspectives, often in ways that make enacting justice difficult, *Disco Elysium* is a game about the mysteries of the self. Who are we truly amid all the things that have happened to us? Is it possible to exist as unique and autonomous beings among all the conflicting and complex ideologies and social perspectives surrounding us? To what extent are our identities always dependent on the specifics of the place and time in which we live? As in *Pentiment*, the solution to the murder in *Disco Elysium* is discoverable, though the story is similarly complex. It is just as easy in *Disco Elysium*, though, to give up on solving the mystery, and there are always unknowable elements, questions that persist despite the best efforts of the investigators. And in the end, the question is less about what solving the mystery means for the community and for history and more about what it means for DuBois himself. Given the game's insistence on the transient fragility of the self, what does it mean to solve a mystery or to fail at solving one? Russell explains that:

> Somewhere near its end you realize *Disco Elysium* is about a broken man working an unworkable case, but also broken people surviving an unworkable world, and the Sisyphean will it takes to see it resolving the way it ought to when you know it likely won't . . . The game can't bring itself to sugarcoat the exhausting pain it reflects, but it leaves you fuller than before. Achingly aware of how there's no destruction from which you cannot rebuild, and that hope will never die.

By giving players the responsibility for shaping DuBois' character and seeing how those choices go on to alter the world, becoming an inescapable lens that colors the narrative, *Disco Elysium* uses meaningful choice, failure, and ideology to highlight the connection between crime and detective, implicating players and making them aware of how their choices alter character, which has a profound impact on justice and the world.

As a game design mechanic, meaningful choice works to implicate players in the narrative experience, giving them a sense of being integral to a story, creating a work that would not exist without their participation. *Pentiment* and *Disco Elysium* illustrate the ways that digital games have the potential to use mystery narratives to raise awareness of contemporary social issues, whether players are watching the ways that their choices spiral outward into historical truths in *Pentiment*, or whether they are making choices that shape DuBois' character and his perspective on the world in *Disco Elysium*. In both cases, players participate in crime narratives happening in worlds very different from their own, while simultaneously being called to examine the forces at work in their own worlds, the ideologies they embrace, the stories they believe, and the alternate viewpoints and perspectives that are possible, and to consider the ways that these choices have shaped who they are and the worlds they live in.

Blurred Boundaries, Cross-Cultural Connections, and Real-World Reflections in *Never Alone, Immortality*, and Transmedia Mysteries

Meaningful choice in digital mystery narratives like *Pentiment* and *Disco Elysium* has the potential to enable players to influence the story, implicating them by allowing them to shape the characters, stories, and world in ways that have profound implications for justice. By making players aware of their impact on the story, particularly in crime narratives, where guilt, culpability, and lawfulness can be complicated, digital games have the potential to encourage players to reflect on their backgrounds and morals, and to consider the political and social systems at work in their own lives. As Rejack notes, modifications and adaptations also give players the opportunity to shape the game world, adapting its emotional experience (noir, in his example) to one of their own. Most games are concerned with fictional characters and worlds, and as I have shown in the previous section, characters and civilizations that are quite different from a player's own can still use interactivity and meaningful choice to encourage players to see their own surroundings and their role in them from a new vantage point. Some games, though, go one step further to use mystery narratives as a way of blurring the boundaries between the fictional world and the real one, or encouraging players to engage with ideology and content with the goal of real-world change. In this section I will explore a variety of games that use mystery narratives to accomplish these goals, with the potential to have a considerable impact on the physical world.

One of the most striking examples of the potential for digital mystery narratives to affect real-world change is the game *Never Alone (Kisima Inŋitchuŋa)*, which was released in 2014. This groundbreaking title was developed through a partnership between Cook Inlet Tribal Council and E-Line Media with the intent of documenting and passing on the cultural traditions and heritage of the Iñupiat people, an indigenous community with traditional territorial roots in Alaska and Canada. The game's website explains that *Never Alone* is "the first game developed in collaboration with the Iñupiat, an Alaska Native people. Nearly 40 Alaska Native elders, storytellers and community members contributed to the development of this game." The game's story is based on traditional Iñupiaq folklore and mythology, and follows a young girl, Nuna, and her arctic fox companion as she travels through tundra, ice floes, an abandoned coastal village, and other Alaskan settings, avoiding polar bears and other environmental and mythological dangers, to solve the mystery of a blizzard that is plaguing her people. In addition to graphics and visuals based on scrimshaw and other traditional Iñupiaq art, the game is heavily rooted in Iñupiaq culture, with the intent of preserving this heritage and sharing it with players.

As players progress through the story, they unlock "Cultural Insight" videos, where elders and other community members explain concepts important to Iñupiaq culture, such as the significance of storytelling, the bola, the importance of paying attention to nature, and environmental changes happening in the region due to climate change. In the "Behind the Scenes" video, Jana Pausauraq Harcharek, Director of Iñupiaq Education, describes the reasons for making the game, explaining that "with the passing of each elder, they take with them lots of pieces of . . . knowledge that perhaps none of us will ever know. Changes have come so fast, and we have become so ingrained in Western media. We're not producing our own to present who we are and the way we view the world from our perspective." In addition to telling an engaging story, the creation of *Never Alone* was motivated by the pressures of a vanishing culture, with the hope that by creating a video game they would pass on important heritage and traditions to young people with less exposure to traditional customs, and the game would further act to raise global awareness of this endangered society. The game's website further describes the goals and approach of the project, explaining,

> We paired world class game makers with Alaska Native storytellers and elders to create a game which delves deeply into the traditional lore of the Iñupiat people to present an experience like no other. *Never Alone* is our first title in an exciting new genre of 'World Games' that draw fully upon the richness of unique cultures to create complex and fascinating game worlds for a global audience.

Thus, the game's goals are weighty and the stakes high.

Not only did creators develop *Never Alone* as a way of perpetuating and sharing Iñupiat heritage with others, but the game is part of a larger aim to create digital games rooted in global indigenous cultures, with the intent to share them with the world. In the book *Gaming at the Edge: Sexuality and Gender at the Margins of Gamer Culture*, Adrienne Shaw explores the complexities of representation in gaming, arguing that deep engagement with a particular culture or perspective tends to be more impactful than tokenism, and that "cultural producers of any sort must be willing to risk a lack of identification in order to get at deeper identification" (226). Further, Shaw argues that rather than "talk about representation's importance in terms of its effect on out-group or in-group members, on the educative or the marketing potential of diversity, a better argument for representation can be made by focusing on the way diverse media gives us the space to imagine the world differently" (11). Thus, by allowing a deep engagement with Iñupiat culture and worldview, *Never Alone* not only gives audiences an insight into experiences that may be different than their own but also encourages them to view the world in a new, distinct way.

Never Alone takes place in a variety of outdoor settings common to the Alaskan wilderness, as players guide Nuna and her fox companion across ice floes and along arctic cliffs, through abandoned villages and forests, on a quest to determine what is causing the blizzard threatening Nuna's village. As a puzzle-platform game, the gameplay is more action-oriented than some of the others discussed in this Element, and players switch between controlling Nuna and the fox to navigate the puzzles. (In a multiplayer game, each player controls one character, and both work together.) Players run from polar bears and navigate challenging jumps across slippery ice. It's common for players to miss a platform and fall into chasm, or to move too slowly, so that the characters are caught by a polar bear or another antagonist. Progressing through the game means avoiding death, and when characters die, players restart the level from an earlier point and try again.

Playstyle is more active and less narrative focused than in the titles previously discussed, but still the game is steeped in legend. Not only is the story based on traditional Iñupiat folklore, but the graphics are influenced by indigenous art common in scrimshaw and inspired by the natural beauty of the region. As players move through the levels, they learn mechanics closely associated with Iñupiat culture and linked to the environment such as bracing against the wind, or timing jumps to gain extra lift from its power. Throughout the story, Nuna and the fox face antagonists common in Iñupiat folklore such as the Terrible One who destroys Nuna's village, the green aurora spirits who are eager to capture Nuna and the fox and carry them to their deaths, and the colossal ice giant at the end of the game who is causing the blizzard by hacking at the ice with a massive adze. Further, the Cultural Insights videos draw analogies between the challenges facing Nuna and her village and those the region is currently facing due to climate change. In this way, the central mystery of the game spans the environmental and the spiritual, drawing on traditional history while also bridging folklore with more contemporary social and cultural concerns.

Most notable about *Never Alone*, however, is its use of procedural rhetoric throughout the narrative. Beyond learning about the culture and history of the Iñupiat people as they complete the levels, completing the game successfully requires players to actively participate in the Iñupiat philosophies and perspectives described in the videos they unlock. Iñupiat elders explain the importance of paying attention to nature, of working with its patterns and listening to its messages, and as Nuna and the fox, players must pay attention to these messages and act in accordance with these teachings to complete the level, learning how to gauge the slipperiness of the ground or the buoyancy of an ice floe. Throughout the Cultural Insights videos, community members talk about the connectedness of the spirit world and the physical one, and in the game, players must learn how to interact with the spirit helpers frequently to solve puzzles in each level. Further, late in the game, the fox is killed in a tragic moment, but rather than disappearing from the game, he becomes a spirit himself, taking the form of a spirit boy who continues to help Nuna on her quest. Not only does the narrative reinforce the beliefs and perspectives presented in the insight videos, but as players have already been trained to rely on the fox for help solving the levels, they continue to do so, not only relying on the spirit world for help, but also actively participating in it when playing as the fox character. The game's playstyle, which has trained players (in a single-player game, at least) to switch between Nuna and the fox in order to progress through the challenges of each level, not only highlights the interconnectedness described in the videos, but requires players to practice that ideology themselves if they hope to succeed.

Beyond conveying information or sharing an important cultural narrative, *Never Alone* requires players to participate in the cultural ideologies and perspectives it depicts. It is impossible to be successful in the game without paying attention to nature, understanding the interactions between the spirit world and the real one, or learning the techniques for throwing a bola. In this way, players must step into important Iñupiat cultural perspectives, joining and sharing in them rather than simply watching them from the outside. By asking players to take on the role of Nuna to solve the mystery of the blizzard, the game passes on a well-known cultural story, while also encouraging players to participate in it. Even if the landscape and cultural traditions are unfamiliar and distant from a player's own, they have still contributed to the story, working to solve its problems. Tracy Fullerton uses the term "flow" to explain the ways that completing a challenging activity often creates emotional connection between a player and game. An effective game, "balances a person between challenge and ability, frustration and boredom, to produce an experience of achievement and happiness" (Fullerton 99). Further, by linking the natural destruction in the narrative to the global pressures of climate change, an overwhelming threat which is as confusing in our own experience as it is in the game, *Never Alone* draws on a common fear, encouraging empathy and connection between players and Iñupiat culture, while also issuing a call to action. Players may not be Nuna in their everyday lives, and they may not be familiar with the arctic wilderness, but the mysteries of climate change impact all of us, and fighting against them is a quest we share, a particularly important one for vulnerable arctic communities such as the Iñupiat.

In this way, *Never Alone* uses its story to pass on cultural information and cultivate empathy and cultural connection. Beyond that, players must actively participate in the cultural ideologies as they learn about them, adopting these viewpoints and perspectives and making them, at least temporarily, their own. Further, by drawing upon shared concerns about climate change, the game makes a larger argument about everyday mysteries and problems facing the planet, a strategy that encourages connection and action. In this example, game design techniques augment the interactive elements of mystery narratives, utilizing procedural ideology to create a play experience with a powerful message and the potential for fostering lasting change in the everyday world.

By foregrounding its goals and the potential for the game to have real-world impact, *Never Alone*, highlights the ways that mystery narratives can foster overt connections between players and cultural experiences that might be unfamiliar. Even transmedia digital narratives without the aim of evoking concrete change, however, can use mystery stories to blur the boundaries between the fictional world and the real one, encouraging players to interact with the world differently, or to consider their everyday surroundings from a new perspective. In *Convergence Culture*, Jenkins uses the example of *The Matrix* to define the term transmedia and explain its relevance to contemporary entertainment culture. Transmedia stories can take a variety of forms, but they are broadly defined as stories that take place across multiple media platforms allowing audiences to enter into and engage with broad fictional worlds in a variety of ways. Within the *Star Wars* franchise, for example, audiences might first learn about the world through watching the popular films, or they might begin with the television series, *The Mandalorian*, or watch the animated series, *Star Wars: Clone Wars*. Beyond television and film, audiences might come to the world through other media, too, by reading novels, playing a tabletop or digital game, or reading a comic or graphic novel. Each media element tells a complete story and stands on its own as an entertainment experience, but taken together, these elements contribute to a deep fictional world that rewards continual engagement. Jenkins explains:

> In the ideal form of transmedia storytelling, each medium does what it does best – so that a story might be introduced in a film, expanded through television, novels, and comics; its world might be explored through game play or experienced as amusement park attraction. Each franchise needs to be self-contained so you don't need to have seen the film to enjoy the game, and vice versa. Any given product is a point of entry into the franchise as a whole. Reading across media sustains a depth of experience that motivates more consumption. (96)

In this way, transmedia narratives encourage interactivity, as audiences are free to choose which elements to engage with and in which order. As in digital games, this sense of choice and agency helps audiences to feel a sense of ownership and involvement, deepening engagement with the story.

Transmedia stories like *Star Wars* and *The Matrix* illustrate the increasing importance of collective intelligence, as it is difficult for any single person to have the cognitive capacity to keep track of so many elements (or even experience all of them), thus this type of storytelling encourages social connections and collaboration, often through online platforms such as websites and forums. This social element, particularly when combined with the puzzle-solving common to mystery stories, has the potential for considerable impact. Jenkins notes the increased role that the audience plays in shaping the story, explaining that "artists are building a more collaborative relationship with their consumers: working together, audience members can process more story information than previously imagined. To achieve these goals, these storytellers are developing a more collaborative model of authorship" (96). Creating stories in this way enables audiences to participate in a narrative, while also giving them considerable responsibility for perpetuating it, both through solving puzzles and engagement, and as a result, narratives told across multiple platforms may look much differently than stories told in more traditional formats.

Jenkins explains the tendency for contemporary works to expect more from audiences in terms of outside engagement, writing, "the old Hollywood system depended on redundancy to ensure that viewers could follow the plot at all times … The new Hollywood demands that we keep our eyes on the road at all times, and that we do research before we arrive at the theater" (104). Increasingly, social interaction becomes a crucial element of narrative engagement, as it is challenging in a transmedia world for any one audience member to keep track of all the narrative components, characters, and worldbuilding elements needed to fully understand a work. In the case of *The Matrix*, Jenkins explains that "across a range of fan sites and discussion lists, the fans were gathering information, tracing allusions, charting chains of command, constructing timelines, assembling reference guides, transcribing dialogue, extending the story through their own fan fiction, and speculating like crazy about what it all meant" (127). Far from being a by-product or a peripheral result, social engagement and community development are crucial to transmedia narrative experience, interwoven and intertwined with the story itself.

As an example of the ways that transmedia storytelling has the potential to impact the experience of mystery narratives, consider the alternate reality game *The Muse*, which took place from 2021 to 2023 across a variety of internet websites and platforms, most notably through YouTube videos. Created by actor Alex Bale, ostensibly as a series of conspiracy videos about the television series *SpongeBob SquarePants*, *The Muse* began with a series of short clips that appeared at the end of Bale's conspiracy videos showing him conversing with a mysterious entity in his garage. Through the course of the narrative, audiences learned that this entity, Bale's "muse," was responsible for his new internet fame, feeding him ideas for conspiracy videos and exacting payments of raw meat and other sacrifices in return. Through the course of the narrative, audiences worked together, deciphering clues in the videos and exploring the internet, eventually uncovering other popular online content creators, each with their own muses, and learning more about the insidious consequences faced by Bale and others whose fame came through the intervention of a "muse."

Captivated by questions about what a muse was and where it came from, audiences eventually followed clues to a fictional animal farming company, Happy Meat Farms, where they discovered links between the muse and the horrible biological experiments conducted by the company. By uncovering codes and inputting them into a simulated employee portal located on the company website, audiences gained access to a series of videos of mutated creatures created by failed experiments, as well as company characters with inside knowledge about the links between the company's insidious goals and the influence of the muse. As a transmedia narrative, *The Muse* encouraged players to work together, watching materials closely for details and clues that might link to further pieces of the puzzle. They might scour Bale's videos, vigilant for names of characters or companies to search for online in hopes they would lead to other parts of the narrative. The story took place in real time, and audiences communicated with one another through online comments and forums, sharing discoveries, and scrutinizing a variety of websites, character profiles, and platforms as they worked to solve the mystery of what was happening to Bale and the others.

The narrative experience in this type of example is quite different from that in more traditional media. For one thing, the story itself appeared initially as a secret, a mysterious clip at the end of a *SpongeBob* conspiracy video. In alternate reality game design, the term "rabbit hole" is used to describe the experience of presenting players with a mystery, a strange detail that, when looked at more closely, pulls audiences into the deeper realm of the story

(Montola 62). In this way, players are asked to place themselves into the role of the detective, tasked with the choice to investigate by looking more closely at a strange occurrence in the seemingly everyday world. Though most players are aware of the fictional nature of the story, they participate in the story as themselves, engaging with other players by commenting on videos, visiting Reddit sites and online forums, and working to solve clues. Unlike a mystery told in a more traditional format, in an alternate reality game, there is very little boundary between the narrative and the real world. The story happens constantly, with players in different geographical locations working perpetually to unravel the secrets. New content can be released or discovered at any time, and characters from the story may communicate with audiences at any point, which contributes to the feeling of the mystery being persistent and pressing, often asking audiences to view their everyday surroundings from a new perspective. In the case of *The Muse*, for example, the story encourages players to look more closely at popular internet content creators, to consider who might be potentially influenced by a muse, and to think more carefully about industrial farming practices and genetic modification. Players are (usually) aware that the story is fictional, but participating in it has the potential for real-world impact as players interact with one another, developing social connections they might not otherwise, and engaging with the world differently, seeing it through the lens of the story, in ways that may persist long after the narrative has ended.

This blurring of boundaries between the fictional and real worlds is common in digital mystery narratives, often with the result of pulling players into the story more deeply, asking them to look more closely at everyday (often digital) experiences, encouraging them to develop social connections or to engage with online community platforms, and asking players to adopt a sense of agency toward the narrative. For instance, in Sam Barlow's 2015 interactive film video game *Her Story*, players must type search terms into a simulated 1990s-era media platform to locate clips from a series of fictional police interviews. By paying close attention to spoken dialogue and clues, players work to locate as many videos as possible to solve the mystery of a missing man and his wife's potential involvement. Barlow's 2022 interactive film game, *Immortality*, takes a similar approach, asking players to use a simulated platform to hunt through a series of video clips, clicking on objects and rewinding to access secret clips hidden within the film footage to solve the mystery of a vanished actor and her three unreleased films. As with the strategies used in transmedia alternate reality games, Barlow's games ask players to enter a crime narrative without fully understanding the scope of it. In these examples, the events of the story are embedded, but scattered, and the games' design strategies encourage players to think deeply and creatively about the ways they use the simulated digital platforms to uncover key elements of the story. In this way, players become detectives, responsible for investigating a crime narrative which will have no solution or ending without their participation. Players must look closely, solve puzzles, and piece events together, and, in a narrative which offers little in the way of guidance or hints, turn to online community resources for help when needed.

Narratives in these examples work similarly to those told through environmental storytelling in that players are asked to explore while looking closely and piecing together clues, but the key difference here is that in transmedia alternate reality games and digital mystery narratives like Barlow's, the environment that the player is exploring is some element of their own, whether it is a simulated search platform that mimics an experience they might have on a streaming platform, or the actual internet they engage with every day. When paired with mystery narratives, this type of storytelling has the effect of asking us to look more closely at our own world, considering the mysteries that might be right in front of our faces, and encouraging us to be more open to the potential for mystery and the unknown in our day-to-day lives.

Even in linear stories, where players have influence on how the story unfolds or how it progresses, simply using a digital platform to tell a story and asking players to view that technology in a new way can implicate players in the narrative and ask them to consider their own digital experiences from a new perspective. Simogo's 2013 release, *Device 6*, for instance, is a digital narrative that takes place on a player's own iPhone or tablet. The story relies significantly on text, and the words twist and turn, requiring players to adjust their phones as they read through the story of a young woman, Anna, who was woken up in an unfamiliar castle, with a vague memory of a strange doll, and is struggling to solve the mystery of what has happened to her. The narrative also incorporates visual and logistical puzzles, and players must scroll through the text, adjusting their devices to help Anna solve them.

Throughout the game, though, players are asked to participate in surveys about the game experience, with questions such as "Which of these shapes do you think describes the previous chapter?" and to interact with their phones in other physical ways, such as by placing it on a flat surface. In his talk, "It's All on You: Implicative Storytelling in Digital Narratives," Tony R. Magagna describes the ways that the storytelling approach in *Device 6* implicates players, by requiring them to interact with their own devices in prescribed ways. Players may think they are outside observers, helping Anna solve the mystery and advancing the story, but by the end of the game, they learn that they are actually the next subject, following Anna in a complex experiment being conducted through player's phone. The help they have offered Anna has awarded them the prize of a strange doll, which will be mailed to them and imprison them in turn. In this way, solving the mystery extends beyond the barriers of the story, implicating players and centering them in the narrative through the common experience of engaging with their mobile device. In this way, *Device 6* tells two stories simultaneously: a fictional narrative about a woman lost in a castle, and another meta-narrative about a player who has endangered themselves by allowing themselves to be controlled by instructions on their phone. Beyond telling a compelling story, *Device 6* further puts players in the position to enact the very relationship with their phones that the game critiques, using real-world interaction to implicate players in a powerful argument about the common tendency to engage mindlessly with our phones.

Device 6 and the other games described in this section use mystery narratives to encourage players to engage with the world differently, pushing them to see things from new perspectives, adopt ideologies and approaches that might be unfamiliar to them, engage with other players and familiar digital technologies in new ways, or impact real-world change. Whether, like *Never Alone*, a game seeks to raise consciousness and empathy for a vanishing culture, or as in transmedia narrative like *The Muse* or a mobile game like *Device 6*, a game blurs the boundaries, linking fiction with day-to-day "reality," implicating players in the narrative and pushing them to consider familiar experiences from a new perspective, there is a great potential for digital narratives to impact players on a meta-level, beyond the fictional boundaries of the story itself. As a genre, crime narratives, which often, as Goldman argues, encourage readers to participate by studying clues alongside the detective and working to develop their own theories of what has happened, are particularly well suited for this kind of narrative impact.

Conclusions and Implications: What the Narrative Strategies of Digital Crime Narratives Mean for Storytelling

Throughout this Element, I have argued that an understanding of game studies concepts and game design techniques helps to illuminate the unique narrative effects possible in digital crime narratives. It's worth noting that there are further techniques and approaches far beyond the scope of this Element. I've focused, for instance, on full-length mystery games, but game narratives outside the genre may still use the mystery format to a smaller extent through side quests or other tangential storylines as a way of pulling players into a deeper relationship with the broader narrative. This Element has also not touched on the unique affordances of mystery narratives told through augmented reality or virtual reality, nor has it touched on procedurally generated mystery games, such as GR3 Project's *La-Mulana* or Mark R. Johnson's *Ultima Ratio Regum*, and other myriad approaches to the genre. Whether games rely on the magic circle to ask players to engage with complex topics in new ways, use environmental storytelling to encourage players to develop empathy and connection to a world and its characters, incorporate meaningful choice to create a sense of player responsibility for the narrative, use proceduralism, or blur the boundaries between the fictional world and the real world to encourage players to see the everyday differently, digital narratives offer a variety of approaches and techniques that are difficult to replicate in other media. In this concluding section, I will argue that an understanding of game studies and game design principles is not only necessary for analyzing the narrative impact of digital works, but that these concepts are also invaluable for understanding storytelling strategies at work in print mystery fiction as well.

As I have explained in this Element's opening, the digital game industry is lucrative, popular, and easily the fastest-growing entertainment focus in the contemporary world. Audiences are increasingly likely to encounter memorable stories within the realm of a digital game, and the popularity of game narratives that have been remade as films or television series – consider *The Witcher*, *The Last of Us*, *Fallout*, and more – has ensured that even audiences who do not consider themselves to be "gamers" are often familiar with these stories. Further, as in the example of *Disco Elysium*, narratives told as digital games may experience greater success and, consequently, have a broader scope than those told in more traditional modes. Beyond comparisons of form, however, these contemporary trends suggest a profound shift in narrative experience and audience expectations, regardless of modality. If audiences are increasingly accustomed to these participatory and interactive narrative experiences, indeed, if they have come to prefer and expect the types of storytelling encounters common in digital games, it is likely that we will see approaches that approximate these experiences becoming more prevalent, even in more traditional print narrative forms. In the remainder of this article, I will illustrate how applying game design concepts and game studies theories to traditional print narratives can help to explain and illuminate the interactive and participatory elements of those texts. This critical approach will likely be enlightening to storytelling experiences in all genres, but it is particularly relevant in the case of mystery narratives, which, as I have explained, have a great deal in common with games to begin with.

In this section, I will illustrate how game studies concepts might be applied to traditional print mystery narratives to more effectively articulate and analyze interactivity than might be possible through conventional literary critical approaches alone. Significant work is still needed in this area, but ideally this section will act as example of how one might approach print mystery novels through the lens of game studies with the effect of illustrating and explicating the ludic elements at work. Early game studies scholars such as Aarseth and Juul explore in detail the ways that traditional literature has always employed the interactive techniques common in games. Often, though, game studies scholars have dismissed these techniques as experimental, unsuccessful, or somehow at odds with the linearity assumed crucial for successful storytelling. In this section, I suggest that in the contemporary world, where games and digital narratives are rapidly becoming the norm for storytelling experiences, that such so-called "experimental," nonlinear techniques are no longer outliers, but have become common and expected within print literature as well. Thus, an understanding of the ways that game studies principles help to illuminate the narrative elements in digital games can prove useful beyond the realm of video games, in print literature as well, by offering a developed and established vocabulary for describing ludic elements and interactivity at work in a text.

John Darnielle's 2022 novel, *Devil House*, is a strong example of a crime narrative with interactive elements that can benefit from the developed vocabulary of game studies analysis. Darnielle's novel is told from the perspective of Gage Chandler, a crime writer who has moved to Milpitas, California, in order to write a book about "Devil House," which is a former pornography store, and the site of two unsolved murders in 1986. The author of the book *The White Witch of Morro Bay*, a true-crime story about a high school teacher who killed two students in self-defense, Chandler, purchases and moves into the Devil House, hoping to learn the truth behind the murders and recreate the success of his previous books. Chandler insists on the importance of slipping into the crime and learning about its participants to understand the story. Early in the novel, Chandler introduces himself in what seems to be a straightforward presentation, explaining, "my name is Gage Chandler. I've been here for almost a year. I moved into this house to tell a story: to employ my usual and usually successful methods to the task. To inhabit the carapace of the crime scene, to retrace the steps of the killer in order to know his path" (67). Despite this seeming forthrightness and commitment to the truth, Darnielle complicates Chandler's relationship to the crime throughout the novel, as he re-creates the scene, gradually painting the house the color it was at the time of the murders, for instance, and working meticulously to re-create the "satanic" elements of the scene, such as the broken glass and strange artifacts on the front lawn. Such details encourage readers to question Chandler's objectivity, and to read between the lines of the novel in search of a more complex truth.

Beyond asking readers to look more closely for clues to what might be going on, a technique common for crime narratives, Darnielle employs interactive elements throughout the text to further draw in and implicate readers. First, several sections are written using the second-person pronoun "you," as Chandler seemingly attempts to understand important people involved in the crimes he is describing, a technique which essentially asks readers to inhabit the text as avatars. In one instance, readers are asked to take on the identity of Diana Crane, the high school teacher who was convicted of murdering two teenagers in Morro Bay. In another, "you" is used for Jana Perez, the mother of one of the murdered high school students, who has written Chandler a lengthy letter asking him to consider the long-term impact that his work has on the people it describes. In both cases, readers are asked to step into skins of the people Chandler writes about, empathizing with them while also acknowledging Chandler's role in creating these characters, raising questions about the capacity for crime writers to convey the truth or perceive it objectively. Darnielle emphasizes the responsibility that writers play in forming a story and the ways that such processes shape all those involved. Chandler reflects, "What happens when somebody tells a story that has real people in it? What happens to the story; what happens to the teller; what happens to the people?" (300). Although Chandler does not inquire about the reader specifically in this list of questions, the use of the second-person pronouns implicates readers in that process as well.

Although the plot of the story proceeds fairly linearly as Chandler works to uncover the true story of what happened at the Devil House, the structural approach of Darnielle's novel invites interactivity as well. Some sections of the novel are told from Chandler's perspective, but in addition to the second-person sections described earlier, other sections approach the story in third person from the perspective of important characters, such as Derrick, Seth, Angela, and Alex, teenagers who were spending time at Devil House during the time of the murders, or Evelyn Gates and Marc Buckler, the victims. Often Chandler intrudes on these dramatizations, which highlights his role in developing these personas and invites readers to ask questions about the nature of their creation. To what extent should we trust what Chandler is telling us? How much of these imagined events is accurate? Jesper Juul defines the term "incoherent" in *Half-Real*, arguing that "in an incomplete fictional world, there are blanks that the player must fill in, an incoherent world *prevents* the player from filling in the blanks" (132). Darnielle's novel never arrives at a clear central storyline; instead, the reader is left with a series of incoherent and conflicting accounts, which are impossible to reconcile. Further, the novel also incorporates artifacts, including a mock cover for *The White Witch of Morro Bay* at the beginning of the work, complete with an illustration of a woman, presumably Diana Crane, half of her face young, the other aged and wrinkled. Toward the middle of the book, a section entitled "Song of Gorbonian" tells a mythical legend, and is printed in a medieval font and written in stylized language. Much like environmental storytelling, little is offered in the way of explanation or context for these elements. Instead, readers are expected to look closely, drawing their own conclusions about what these elements mean and how to interpret them in light of the complexities of Chandler's character.

It isn't until the end of the novel that the impact of these narrative choices becomes clear. In the final section of the book, which is told from the perspective of Chandler's childhood friend, we learn that Chandler has fabricated the story of what has happened at Devil House, inventing the cast of characters we have come to connect with, and completely obscuring the truth of the actual crime. Chandler tells his friend, "Once I started messing with the details it felt like it wouldn't matter if I moved a few of the principal players around. Nobody cares about the actual details of anything, they just want the feeling they get when the story punches their buttons" (398). Although the true details of the crime remain unclear, the final section of the book suggests that Chandler developed the false story in an effort to protect the true killers, transient adults who were using the abandoned store as their home. Chandler tells his friend, "It matters which story you tell, it matters whose story you tell, it matters what people think . . . We don't see the gigantic expanse over there on the other side of the flames, but, you know. People have to *live* there" (402). In this way, Darnielle uses the interactive elements of the text as a kind of proceduralism, asking readers to actively participate in creating meaning, reading between the lines to decipher the truth, and ultimately implicating them in that process. *Devil House* is, finally, a book about the tyranny of reading and storytelling, asking readers to consider the ways that their own expectations and desires shape stories, resulting in obscured truth and destroyed lives. The interactive elements blur the boundaries between the fictional world and the real one, implicating readers by asking them to consider their own role in the process.

Louise Erdrich employs a similar technique in her 2021 novel, *The Sentence*, which tells the story of an Ojibwe woman, Tookie, an ex-convict and an employee at a Minneapolis bookstore who is haunted by the ghost of Flora, a former customer who died while reading an unusual book. Flora, referred to throughout as "one of [the bookstore's] most annoying customers" (32), is an older white woman who insists on her indigenous heritage, frequenting the bookstore and badgering its indigenous employees, learning crafts such as beadwork, and attending local powwows and other native events. Flora haunts the bookstore and Tookie, in particular, shuffling among the aisles, flinging books to the ground, and at one point, even trying to take possession of Tookie's body.

The novel's central mystery focuses on Flora's death and afterlife desires, and at the end of the book Tookie learns that the thing that killed Flora was the realization that she does not in fact have indigenous heritage, but that she is instead the descendent of a "woman who was known for keeping other women locked in a bedroom. This woman ran what was called 'a house of commercial affection.' She rented out these women's bodies and was known to have covered up or perhaps committed several murders" (344). Tookie realizes that in reading that sentence, "at that instant, Flora's identity turned upside down. Everything that she'd concocted about herself turned out to be its opposite" (345). At the end of the novel, Flora's ghost is exorcised by the bookstore staff, who offer her forgiveness, and the book highlights several instances of white people, mainly women, who seem intent on celebrating their own open-mindedness and support of indigenous communities, while seemingly unaware of harmful consequences of their actions. Though Flora's ghost is offered forgiveness by the book story employees and the indigenous characters who knew her, as a whole, the novel presents the complexities of these white characters with limited empathy, representing them as oblivious, un-examined, and a constant emotional burden on the indigenous characters who are compelled to interact with them. Tookie's life is upended by Flora's ghost, who, in the course of her haunting, literally attempts to inhabit Tookie's body, illustrating the ways that colonization and discrimination can have a persistent, devastating impact beyond historical and political systems, on a personal and spiritual level.

Beyond its critique of white saviorism and indigenous fetishization, though, Erdrich's novel raises questions about identity and guilt, resisting easy answers and categorization. Early in the novel, Tookie begins reading the book that killed Flora and has a near-death experience herself. She says, "I felt my body disintegrating in a cascade of cells. My thoughts bleeding into the obliterating gray. I saw my atoms spinning off like black snow into the air of my bedroom" (84). Tookie does not share what she has read or explain its effect until the end of the novel, when she reveals that she was named after Flora, who kept Tookie's drug-addicted mother sober while she was pregnant, and that she may owe Flora her life. These complicated connections between characters are common throughout the novel, and they make it difficult to categorize characters or their relationship to one another. Tookie's husband, Pollux, for instance, is an affectionate, supportive presence throughout the novel, but he is also a former police officer, and the person who arrested Tookie and sent her to jail. The book takes place during the time of the Minneapolis riots that happened in response to the murder of George Floyd, and in navigating the political events of the city, Tookie also finds herself excavating and navigating feelings of distrust for Pollux. While trying to understand the anger that has risen toward him due to the riots, Tookie sees, "my fingers open, ready to wind with [Pollux's] fingers, but instead he cuffs me up. Well, he didn't use cuffs, to be real about it, he used a zip tie like you'd fasten on a bag of garbage" (257). Much in the way that the sentence Flora read forced her to see herself and her identity in a new light, the political events happening in Minneapolis push Tookie to unearth and reexamine the implications of her own sentence, and the ways it has shaped her relationship with Pollux and her own sense of self.

Many characters in the novel struggle to reconcile their experiences and past actions into a sense of cohesive identity. Though Pollux is clearly dedicated to maintaining the peace and protecting citizens, the riots bring him face to face with the complicated reality of being an indigenous police officer in a time when people of color are frequent victims of police brutality. In a section entitled "The Haunting of Pollux," Pollux reflects on his grandmother's response the first time she saw him in his police uniform, telling him to "'Watch out . . . for when that uniform starts to wear you'" (283). The riots push him to reflect on the ways his experiences as an officer have changed him, and he remembers, "the way he'd hear his voice scratch out an angry order. The simple weariness that gave way to cynical weariness. The impatience with stupid stuff people did that froze his heart. The anger that led to a violent refusal to feel. Then even to connect with his people" (283). The swirl of social and political turmoil affects not only his relationship with Tookie but also his sense of self, and Erdrich presents this reckoning with the past as a kind of haunting. Similarly, Tookie also struggles with her past. As a young woman, she transported a dead body across state lines as a favor to her then-girlfriend, unaware that the man had bags of drugs taped to his body. As she and Pollux discuss Flora and hauntings, Tookie begins to realize the ways that her past treatment of the dead violated indigenous cultural practices, and she is haunted by her actions as well the trauma of being incarcerated. Tookie reflects, "How much do we owe the dead? I supposed that question was my devil" (316). Struggling with the events of the past and Flora's haunting, Tookie grapples with her own guilt and labors to maintain a sense of identity among these complex forces. In this way, Flora's haunting acts as a metaphor for broader questions of identity. In the middle of such contradictory possible senses of self, which perspectives are the true ones?

The text goes further by using interactive elements to draw readers into the text and implicate them in these questions of identity and culpability. *The Sentence* is clearly a work of fiction, yet Erdrich blurs the boundaries between fiction and reality in the text much in the way that digital online transmedia stories do. The novel's characters work at Birchbark Books, an independent bookstore that Erdrich owns herself in Minneapolis. Further, Louise Erdrich appears as herself in the book, interacting frequently with the other characters, and even going on a real-life book tour that is cut short by the Covid-19 pandemic. Erdrich's biographical note informs readers that "a ghost lives in her creaky old house," which further implies that hauntings such as Flora's could be less fantastical than readers might believe. The plot of the book takes place from 2020 to 2021 and is heavily rooted in actual real-life events, such as the pandemic, George Floyd's murder, and the subsequent riots in Minneapolis. As much as the book follows the experiences of specific fictional characters, its close connection to real-life people, places, and shared memorable and traumatic experiences such as the pandemic and the police riots makes it very difficult for readers to fully distance themselves from the events of the text. Much like a transmedia narrative, the blurred boundaries between fiction and the real world pull readers into the text, implicating them in the events of the story and asking them to reflect on their own complex identities and past experiences.

Like *Devil House*, *The Sentence* is also a book concerned with the problematic ramifications of distilling a story and its multiple perspectives into one objective account, and one of its central questions focuses on the power of books, and the potential for something as simple as sentence to kill someone. Throughout the novel, Tookie and her colleagues recommend books to customers and fill orders, so that the novel presents a network of other narratives and perspectives that readers might consider. Books are a lifeline for characters during the pandemic, and Erdrich ends the book with a giant list entitled "Totally Biased List of Tookie's Favorite Books" with categories such as "Ghost-Managing Book List," "Sailboat Table," and "Books for Banned Love." This further blurs the boundaries and situates *The Sentence* as a kind of transmedia narrative, encouraging readers to explore other titles specifically through the lens of Erdrich's novel, not just as books they might like, but as books that might help them better understand Tookie and her experiences in the novel.

The effect of this creates a reading experience that is similar to one that Emily St. John Mandel employs in her novels *The Glass Hotel* and *Sea of Tranquility*. In *The Glass Hotel*, published in 2020, Mandel uses the story of mysterious graffiti in a Vancouver Island Hotel to tell the story of the collapse of an international Ponzi scheme. *Sea of Tranquility*, published in 2022, explores the possibility and implications of time travel, and takes place in multiple time frames, including a section that takes place in 2020 and follows characters from *The Glass Hotel*, including one who is exploring the mysterious disappearance of the character Vincent at the end of the *Glass Hotel*. The time travel narrative of *Sea of Tranquility* expands much further than the events of *The Glass Hotel*, and its storyline is not necessarily reliant on previous knowledge of the book, but for readers who are familiar with Mandel's earlier novel, its references and storylines encourage them to examine and engage with that book from a different perspective, reconsidering its characters and seeing its storyline in a new light. This is clearly transmedia storytelling, but its re-imagining of Mandel's earlier novel also acts as a kind of failure and replay, encouraging readers to re-read in order to reexamine and refine their perspectives on the book. The book lists throughout *The Sentence* create a similar effect, asking readers to explore and revisit titles by indigenous authors and writers of color, and to engage with them through the lens of Erdrich's novel.

Examining *Devil House* and *The Sentence* through the lenses of game design and game studies principles provides a useful and expansive vocabulary for discussing and examining the strategies of interactivity employed by these texts. In both cases, although neither work is engaged with digital technology specifically, both employ strategies designed to involve readers in shaping the meaning of a text, to blur the boundaries between the real world and the fictional one, to question the capacity of a story to convey the complete truth, and to implicate readers in the complex processes of storytelling, with its tendency to silence some voices while amplifying others. Narrative strategies that promote interactivity are nothing new, but in their early evaluations of ergodic literature, game scholars such as Aarseth and Juul might have dismissed such tactics as "experimental" or "novelty," citing them as outliers to more traditional and linear modes of storytelling. Both Darnielle's and Erdrich's books are bestsellers, however, celebrated by audiences from a variety of backgrounds and perspectives. Further, they are part of a long-standing tradition of crime and mystery narratives that have long used interactive strategies and puzzle-solving to engage audiences and involve them in the storytelling process.

It may be tempting to view the analysis of digital mystery games as a broadening of the canon of crime narrative studies, opening the field to make space for a new and popular narrative form. To simply apply literary critical frameworks to these works is to miss the point, however. Without an examination of game studies principles, any analysis of a digital game is incomplete, as it ignores the unique mechanisms afforded by games, allowing creators to implicate players by shaping the story, exploring the environment, or integrating the world of the narrative into their everyday lives. Further, in a world where digital storytelling is rapidly becoming the norm rather than the exception, where technical advancements and burgeoning game industries mean that interactive storytelling experiences are not only more common than ever before, but also continually and rapidly evolving, this is likely only the beginning. Instead of asking what literary studies might bring to game narratives, we should instead ask what game design principles and game studies approaches might illuminate or reveal in our traditional print texts, by providing a deeper and more nuanced vocabulary for interactive narrative strategies. An understanding of game design is crucial for analyzing and discussing the storytelling techniques at work in the present world, regardless of modality. In no genre is this work more relevant or applicable than in the study of contemporary crime fiction.

Works Cited

Aarseth, Espen J. *Cybertext: Perspectives on Ergodic Literature*. Johns Hopkins University Press, 1997.

Anable, Aubrey. *Playing with Feelings: Video Games and Affect*. University of Minnesota Press, 2018.

Arieces. "Retrospect Analysis: *Gone Home*." *Arieces Blog*. December 12, 2013. Accessed August 12, 2017.

Bell, Alice and Astrid Ensslin. *Reading Digital Fiction: Narrative, Cognition, Mediality*. Routledge, 2024.

Bogost, Ian. *Persuasive Games: The Expressive Power of Videogames*. MIT Press, 2007.

    "The Rhetoric of Video Games." In *The Ecology of Games: Connecting Youth, Games, and Learning*. Edited by Katie Salen. The John D. and Catherine T. MacArthur Foundation Series on Digital Media and Learning. MIT Press, 2008, pp. 117–140.

    "Television Is Better without Video Games." *The Atlantic*, January 30, 2023. www.theatlantic.com/technology/archive/2023/01/the-last-of-us-video-game-hbo-show-episode-3/672889/. Accessed July 6, 2023.

    "Video Games Are Better without Stories." *The Atlantic*, 25 April 2017, www.theatlantic.com/technology/archive/2017/04/video-games-stories/524148/ Accessed August 1, 2023.

Caruth, Cathy. *Unclaimed Experience: Trauma, Narrative, and History*. Johns Hopkins University Press, 1996.

Cohen, Jason. "*Pentiment* Review: A Magical Murder Mystery." *PCMAG*, March 24, 2023, www.pcmag.com/reviews/pentiment. Accessed August 17, 2023.

Consalvo, Mia. *Cheating: Gaining Advantage in Videogames*. MIT Press, 2007.

Cullen, Johnny. "How *Journey* Only Truly Made Sense When Almost Everything Had Been Cut." *Eurogamer*, July 8, 2018. www.eurogamer.net/how-journey-only-truly-made-sense-when-almost-everything-had-been-cut Accessed August 11, 2023.

Darnielle, John. *Devil House*. Picador, 2022.

Device 6. iOS Version, Simogo, 2013.

Disco Elysium, discoelysium.com/. Accessed July 5, 2023.

Disco Elysium. Windows PC Version, ZA/UM, 2019.

Ditum, Nathan. "*Firewatch* Review – A Small Game with a Big Story." The Guardian, 8 February 8, 2016. www.theguardian.com/technology/2016/feb/08/firewatch-review-first-person-simulation-adventure-game. Accessed August 16, 2023.

Erdrich, Louise. *The Sentence*. Harper Perennial, 2021.

Fernández-Vara, Clara. "Designing the Mystery: Elision and Exegesis in Games." In *Narratives Crossing Boundaries: Storytelling in a Transmedial and Transdisciplinary Context*, edited by Joachim Friedmann, transcript Verlag, 2023, pp. 49–62.

Firewatch. PlayStation 4 Version, Campo Santo, 2016.

Flanagan, Mary and Helen Nissenbaum. *Values at Play in Digital Games*. MIT Press, 2014.

Fullerton, Tracy. *Game Design Workshop: A Playcentric Approach to Creating Innovative Games*. Boca Raton, FL: CRC Press, 2019.

Genette, Gérard. *Narrative Discourse: An Essay in Method*. Cornell University Press, 1980.

Goldman, Alan H. "The Appeal of the Mystery." *Journal of Aesthetics & Art Criticism*, vol. 69, no. 3, August 2011, pp. 261–272. *EBSCOhost*, https://doi.org/10.1111/j.1540-6245.2011.01470.x.

Gone Home. Windows PC Version, The Fullbright Company, 2013.

Isbister, Katherine. *How Games Move Us: Emotion by Design*. MIT Press, 2016.

Jenkins, Henry. *Convergence Culture: Where Old and New Media Collide*. New York University Press, 2006.

Journey. PlayStation 4 Version, Thatgamecompany, 2012.

Juul, Jesper. *The Art of Failure: An Essay of the Pain of Playing Video Games*. MIT Press, 2013.

   Half-Real: Video Games between Real Rules and Fictional Worlds. MIT Press, 2005.

Knight, Stephen. *Form & Ideology in Crime Fiction*. Indiana University Press, 1980.

Koenitz, Hartmut. "What Game Narrative Are We Talking about? An Ontological Mapping of the Foundational Canon of Interactive Narrative Forms." *Arts (Basel)*, vol. 7, no. 4, 2018, pp. 51–62.

Kopas, Merritt. "On Gone Home." In *Queer Game Studies*, edited by Bonnie Ruberg and Adrienne Shaw, University of Minnesota Press, 2017, pp. 145–150. *JSTOR*, www.jstor.org/stable/10.5749/j.ctt1mtz7kr.18. Accessed February 3, 2024.

La-Mulana. PC Version, GR3 Project, 2006.

Life is Strange. PlayStation 4 Version, Dontnod Entertainment, 2015.

Lopez, German. "Unions and Video Games." *The New York Times*, January 24, 2023, www.nytimes.com/2023/01/24/briefing/game-worker-union.html. Accessed July 5, 2023.

Lorelei and the Laser Eyes. PC Version. Simogo, 2024.

Macklin, Colleen and John Sharp. *Games, Design, and Play: A Detailed Approach to Iterative GameDesign*. Pearson Education, 2016.

Magagna, Tony R. "It's All on You: Implicative Storytelling in Digital Narratives." 33rd International Conference on Narrative, International Society for the Study of Narrative, Montréal, Québec, Canada, April 18–22, 2018. Conference Presentation.

Mandel, Emily St. John. *The Glass Hotel*. Random House, 2020.

Sea of Tranquility. Alfred A. Knopf, 2022.

Mckeown, Conor. "'What Kind of Cop Are You?' *Disco Elysium's* Technologies of the Self within the Posthuman Multiverse." *Baltic Screen Media Review*, vol. 9, no. 1, 2021, pp. 68–79. https://doi.org/10.2478/bsmr-2021-0007.

Minor, Jordan. "Disco Elysium – The Final Cut (for PC) Review." *PC Magazine*, www.pcmag.com/reviews/disco-elysium-the-final-cut-for-pc. Accessed July 5, 2023.

Montola, Markus, Jaakko Stenros and Annika Waern. *Pervasive Games: Theory and Design*. CRC Press, 2009.

Murray, Janet H. *Hamlet on the Holodeck: The Future of Narrative in Cyberspace*. MIT Press, 1997.

Never Alone (Kisima Inŋitchuŋa). http://neveralonegame.com/game/ Accessed August 19, 2023.

Never Alone (Kisima Inŋitchuŋa). PC version. Upper One Games, 2014.

Peel, Jeremy. "An Interview with Fullbright's Steve Gaynor: What Made *Gone Home* Work?" *PC Games*, December 23, 2013. www.pcgamesn.com/indie/interview-fullbrights-steve-gaynor-what-made-gone-home-work. Accessed August 14, 2023.

Penabella, Miguel. "Why Are We so Afraid to Walk?" *Kill Screen*, November 17, 2015, https://killscreen.com/previously/articles/why-are-we-so-afraid-walk. Accessed August 12, 2023.

Pentiment. Steam Deck version, Obsidian Entertainment, 2023.

Rejack, Brian. "Playing with Negativity: Max Payne, Neoliberal Collapse, and the Noir Video Game." In *Noir Affect*, edited by Christopher Breu and Elizabeth A. Hatmaker, Fordham University Press, 2020, pp. 178–196.

Ruberg, Bonnie. *Video Games Have Always Been Queer*. New York University Press, 2019.

Rollings, Andrew and Dave Morris. *Game Architecture and Design: A New Edition*. New Riders Publishing, 2004.

Russell, Laurence. "The Incredible, Absurd World of *Disco Elysium: The Final Cut*." *Wired*, Conde Nast, June 7, 2021. www.wired.com/story/disco-elysium-the-final-cut/. Accessed August 18, 2023.

Salesses, Matt. *Craft in the Real World*. Catapult, 2021.

Shaw, Adrienne. *Gaming at the Edge: Sexuality and Gender at the Margins of Gamer Culture*. University of Minnesota Press, 2014.

Sicart, Miguel. "Against Procedurality." *Game Studies*, vol. 11, no. 3, December 2011. https://gamestudies.org/1103/articles/sicart_ap. Accessed June 11, 2025.

"Play Computers: A Letter to the Reader" Suter, et al. pp. 47–66.

Shibolet, Yotam. "Game Movement as Enactive Focalization." *Press Start.*, vol. 4, no. 2, 2018, pp. 51–71.

Suter, Beat, Mela Kocher and René Bauer, editors. *Games and Rules: Game Mechanics for the "Magic Circle."* Transcript, 2018.

"Rules of Play as a Framework for the 'Magic Circle.'" Suter, et al. pp. 19–34.

Taylor, Ivy. "Chasing Oblivion with *Disco Elysium* and Alcohol Addiction." *GamesIndustry.Biz*, October 31, 2018, www.gamesindustry.biz/disco-elysium. Accessed August 18, 2023.

Tekinbas, Katie Salen and Eric Zimmerman. *Rules of Play: Game Design Fundamentals*. MIT Press, 2003.

Todorov, Tzvetan. "Typology of Detective Fiction." In *Crime and Media: A Reader*, edited by Chris Greer. Routledge, 2010, pp. 138–144.

Turchi, Peter. *A Muse and a Maze: Writing as Puzzle, Mystery, and Magic*. Trinity University Press, 2014.

Ultima Ratio Regum. PC Version, Mark R. Johnson, 2012.

Vella, Daniel and Cielecka, Magdalena. "'You Won't Even Know Who You Are Anymore': Bakthinian Polyphony and the Challenge to the Ludic Subject in *Disco Elysium*." *Baltic Screen Media Review*, vol. 9, no. 1, 2021, pp. 90–104. https://doi.org/10.2478/bsmr-2021-0009.

Wiltshire, Alex, "The Making of *Disco Elysium*: How Za/Um Created One of the Most Original RPGs of the Decade." *Gamesradar*, January 9, 2020, www.gamesradar.com/the-making-of-disco-elysium-how-zaum-created-one-of-the-most-original-rpgs-of-the-decade/. Accessed July 5, 2023.

Cambridge Elements

Crime Narratives

Margot Douaihy
Emerson College

Margot Douaihy, PhD, is an assistant professor at Emerson College in Boston. She is the author of *Scorched Grace* (Gillian Flynn Books/Zando, 2023), which was named one of the best crime novels of 2023 by *The New York Times*, *The Guardian*, and *CrimeReads*. Her recent scholarship includes 'Beat the Clock: Queer Temporality and Disrupting Chrononormativity in Crime Fiction', a NeMLA 2024 paper.

Catherine Nickerson
Emory College of Arts and Sciences

Catherine Ross Nickerson is the author of *The Web of Iniquity: Early Detective Fiction by American Women* (Duke University Press, 1999), which was nominated for an Edgar Award by the Mystery Writers of America. She is the editor of *The Cambridge Companion to American Crime Fiction* (2010), as well as two volumes of reprinted novels by Anna Katharine Green and Metta Fuller Victor (Duke University Press).

Henry Sutton
University of East Anglia

Henry Sutton, SFHEA, is Professor of Creative Writing and Crime Fiction at the University of East Anglia. He is the author of fifteen novels, including two crime fiction series. He is also the author of *Crafting Crime Fiction* (Manchester University Press, 2023), and the co-editor of *Domestic Noir: The New Face of 21st Century Crime Fiction* (Palgrave Macmillan, 2018).

Advisory Board

William Black, *Johns Hopkins University*
Christopher Breu, *Illinois State University*
Cathy Cole, *Liverpool John Moores University and University of Wollongong*
Stacy Gillis, *Newcastle University*
Femi Kayode, *Author (Namibia)*
Richie Narvaez, *Fashion Institute of Technology*
Andrew Pepper, *Belfast University*
Barbara Pezzotti, *Monash University*
Clare Rolens, *Palomar College*
Shampa Roy, *University of Delhi*
David Schmid, *University of Buffalo*
Samantha Walton, *Bath Spa University*
Aliki Varvogli, *University of Dundee*

About the Series

Publishing groundbreaking research from scholars and practitioners of crime writing in its many dynamic and evolving forms, this series examines and re-examines crime narratives as a global genre which began on the premise of entertainment, but quickly evolved to probe pressing political and sociological concerns, along with the human condition.

Cambridge Elements

Crime Narratives

Elements in the Series

Forensic Crime Fiction
Aliki Varvogli

Female Anger in Crime Fiction
Caroline Reitz

Crime Fiction and Ecology: From the Local to the Global
Nathan Ashman

Bloodlines: Adoption, Crime, and the Search for Belonging
Jinny Huh

Writing the Detectives: Character and the Series Form
Elspeth Latimer

Interactivity and Meta-Engagement in Digital Mystery Narratives
Julialicia Case

A full series listing is available at: www.cambridge.org/ECNA

For EU product safety concerns, contact us at Calle de José Abascal, 56–1°, 28003 Madrid, Spain or eugpsr@cambridge.org.

www.ingramcontent.com/pod-product-compliance
Lightning Source LLC
LaVergne TN
LVHW011856060526
838200LV00054B/4368